The Sound of the Snow Geese

Dax Meredith

Copyright © 2018 Dax Meredith
All rights reserved.

All rights reserved, including the right to reproduce this book or portions thereof in any form whatsoever.

Names and identifying details of people included in this book have been changed.

"Refugee"
Words and music by Tom Petty and the Heartbreakers
Copyright © 1980 Jimmy Lovine and Tom Petty

"Just like Fire"
Words and music by Pink, Max Martin, Shellback, and Oscar Holter
Copyright © 2016 RCA and Walt Disney Records

Cover Photography by Rüdiger Wittmann
Copyright © 123rf

ISBN 978-1-7340265-0-4 (pbk)

Dedication

This book is dedicated to my amazing boys. You are my heroes every single day, my joy and light. I love you to infinity.

To my Andy, who put others before himself at such a young age in the face of danger; I could not be prouder. I love you so much.

And to my Tommy, who put aside fear and remembered to pray. I love you baby boy.

Author's Note

Please be advised that this book contains graphic descriptions and intense traumatic events. Plan to read with caution if you have been impacted by a natural disaster or other trauma that may make reading this a trigger for you or cause extreme anxiety. Parental discretion is advised based on your child's maturity level, sensitivity, and life experiences. In general, the recommended age is twelve and up.

Included in the back of the book are a compilation of coping techniques that I encourage everyone to read, whether the information is for you or to help support others around you. My intent with this book is to provide an historical account of real events, instill hope in other survivors, and share the impact of faith during difficult times.

Names have been changed to protect the privacy of survivors and all other individuals mentioned, whether they deserve it or not. Partial proceeds of sales will benefit Camp Fire survivors and disaster relief services to contribute to natural disaster recovery around the world. May God bless and keep you near.

Dax Meredith

Prologue

The Week Before

In the days leading up to what would be one of the deadliest and most destructive fires in history, there were no indicators that we would experience an event more terrifying than was possibly imaginable. There were no unusual signs, no strange events or daunting forecasts that were alarming. And yet the beasts of Hades broke loose on a grouping of small mountain communities in Northern California in a manner in which can only be described as Armageddon-like proportions. Even the graphic news footage, survivor stories of terror, and recurring nightmares and flashbacks don't do it justice. This fire was a living, breathing, all consuming demon from Hell itself. It blasted through towns like a bomb had been detonated. And that's how first responders and fire analysts referred to it in the aftermath: a bomb. How do you evacuate entire towns safely from this type of event? This question was posed to numerous respected experts, and they all basically concluded the same thing. The answer: you don't. This fire took out everything in its wake at an unfathomable speed. CNN posted that It decimated football field sized areas every second for days. That means you can't outrun it. That means you can't outdrive it. That means you can't escape it.

Homes were overtaken, along with roads, stores, cars, people. Gone. The town of Paradise was literally wiped off the map. Drone footage shows a blackened, ashen, barren flatland of what once was an entire town. The images look as if nothing at all could possibly have remained. And yet somehow, miraculously, inexplicably, a group of people huddled together trapped on a small cement slab in that town were able to survive as their worlds went up in flames all around them. My young son and I were in that group, and this is our true story of faith, hope, and resilience.

Here is the official transcript of a computerized female voice message left on my home phone from Pacific Gas and Electric Company: This is an important safety alert from Pacific Gas and Electric Company. Extreme weather conditions and high fire danger are forecasted in Butte County starting this Tuesday, November 6, 2018 and lasting through Saturday, November 10, 2018. These conditions may cause power outages in the area of your address starting with 13000. To protect public safety, PG&E may also temporarily turn off power in your neighborhood or community. If there is an outage, we will work to restore service as soon as it is safe to do so. Please have your emergency plan ready. If you see a downed power line, assume it is energized and extremely dangerous. Do not touch or try to move it and keep children and animals away. Report downed power lines immediately by calling 911. For more information on how to prepare, please visit PGE.com/wildfiresafety or call 1-800-PGE-5002. Thank you.

When I hear the automated voice message, I find it bizarre. They also leave a message indicating that they may potentially cut power for five to ten days. It is still particularly warm for November, but historically there have often been what my grandparents call "Indian Summers" where summer heat waves ripple long into the autumnal months. The summers here are always roasting, with waves peaking well over one hundred degrees each year. The weather does not seem to be much different than other Novembers, except that possibly there has been less rain. I share with family and neighbors that in the case of multiple days without electricity, the boys and I will stay in the nearby city of Chico until power is restored. It's too long to go without air conditioning, lights, hot water, and refrigeration with two young kids and a puppy. We wait, but PG&E never disconnects the electricity. We stay home.

High winds occur all the time in this area. We live up in Magalia, a small, mountainous town nestled in the pines, right up above Paradise. Wind gusts are known to snap the pine trees in half like they are little sticks. People have died from the trees falling because of the high wind speeds. So what is different now? Why would the power be cut this time and not any times previously? It has never been disconnected for this reason in the fifteen years I have lived here. And the winds won't last five to ten days. Because of this I find PG&E's high wind advisory very odd, as do most of my neighbors.

It's unfortunate, tragic really, that PG&E never did cut the power. Later it is released publicly that a neglected transmission tower and power lines were very likely the cause of the fire. In addition, PG&E apparently knew ahead of time that the transmitter was faulty and sparking, sending out an email to a woman named Betsy who owns the property that holds the transmitter which was in all probability responsible for the start of the mass destruction. The email was regarding repairs, and indicated sparking was occurring. It was sent out the day prior to the fire. PG&E also publicly announced that problems were occurring with power lines in the area a few minutes before the fire began. Cal Fire has since been able to confirm that the fire did start in approximately that same area on Betsy's property. I was also informed by attorneys conducting an investigation that even six hours into the fire starting, PG&E still had not shut down power. It will take over six months for Cal Fire to conclude their investigation and publicly post their findings.

Chapter 1

All the forces of darkness cannot stop what God has ordained.

Isaiah 14:27

6:32 a.m.

I have two young boys; Andy is eleven and Tommy just turned nine. They are the most amazing young people imaginable, and are my indescribable joy, my sunshine, the lights of my world. Our time together is precious, and even at their ages they already know it. I battled a devastatingly long term illness three years ago, and they battled it with me. Helped me to fight. Helped me to live. Were my reasons why for everything, a billion times over. We are grateful for every single day, even the rough ones, which still plague our family. So far, this particular day seems to be going fine, with only one small, foreseeable challenge before us. Thankfully, it is nothing too far out of the ordinary.

Today is a peaceful and beautiful Thursday morning in November, and the three of us cuddle in my huge bed in the early hours of the dawn, silently lamenting that it isn't quite yet the weekend. We love our weekends, especially the cooler mornings spent sleeping in, buried under the heavy Sherpa like comforter. We embrace lounging around in pajamas way later than is considered acceptable in any culture. My youngest calls them pajama days, and they are fantastic.

Typically we would normally already be out of bed and getting ready for school, but we didn't sleep well last night, and I hit snooze on the alarm a few times. It dings at us until I finally manage to slap it, missing twice before making contact. Andy, my oldest, came down with a flu bug yesterday and still has a fever. This is always a concern as he tends to get spike fevers and might need medical attention if it gets too high. I am off work today, and can stay home with him to watch it. We snuggle deeper into the blankets and I pray my thanks for this sweet moment. Warm snuggles with my babes. I hit snooze yet again and then reach over Andy for the phone, and call in to his school down in the nearby city of Chico to report his absence. I then call my mom and ask her to drive Tommy to school, so that Andy can stay home with me and rest in bed. She immediately agrees to come help us, and drives over to our place to pick up Tommy, helping him to remember his backpack, lunch, and hoodie. Before they leave, he runs into my room, crawls up on the bed, and gives me a sweet kiss goodbye. Just as I open my eyes from the kiss, he's off the bed and out of sight.

"Love loves," he yells, running down the hall.

"Love you baby!" I call out to his back. The front door slams shut, and then they are gone; the morning quiet in the house again with only the soft sounds of the leaves rustling outside. They take off just like it is a normal day. Just like it is part of our routine. Just like the biggest issue today will only be watching Andy's fever and being a little sleep deprived. Just like a mother's worst nightmare isn't about to happen.

8:37 a.m.

I am still in bed with Andy and check his fever again. The thermometer slides across his forehead, scans, beeps. The digital screen shows 101.2. I check it again, because I'm like that with my kids, especially when they are ill. I always double check. *Slide, scan, beep.* 101.4. It is still low, still manageable. I give him a dose of Motrin to help fight the fever off and keep it down, keep it under control. We don't need any stress today, don't need any surprises. We just need to spend today in bed and on the couch, cuddling, resting, napping. Maybe watch a movie later. I snuggle back into the pillows, with Andy's too warm body pressed against mine. I'm just about to fall back asleep and make up for the long night when the phone rings. I groggily answer, and hear my mom on the line. I catch bits and pieces of her voice as the call breaks in and out. "Huge plume of smoke. Ugly. Maybe plan to evacuate."

The call drops. I wait two minutes and she calls back with better reception. She tells me that she has dropped off Tommy already and is now heading back to her place, and sees the smoke from a fire up in the hills. She is going back home in case she has to evacuate later. The fire is up in Jarbo Gap, quite a distance from her property, but we know not to take any chances. Here we go again, I think. These damn wildfires. Every summer and into early fall. Another year, another evacuation. We have been through it before and know what to do, know what to expect. This fire is towns and towns away. I take a moment to pray for them.

There have been much closer fires in the past, much more of a threat to us than this. I begin to mentally prepare for a potential evacuation anyway, even though my place is much further away than my mom's. Just to be extra cautious. I am not one to take chances when it comes to safety. We can always unpack everything later, it isn't the first time. It happens every year. Someone sparks a fire, or multiple spot fires, we evacuate when needed and wait for containment. It's routine by now. At this point I do not panic in the least. At this point I am not even nervous. At this point I am still under the false impression that I am in control and we are not in danger.

I make some calls to my neighbors, aunt, cousin, and grandmother to alert them to be on watch and recommend they prepare to evacuate, again, just to be on the safe side. I toss some overnight items into a bag, in case we opt to stay overnight down in Chico until the fire is contained. Some pajamas, socks, a few pairs of underwear. It never hurts to have extra underwear, I think to myself, though I might even say it out loud. I chuckle at this. Goodness gracious, when did I become my mother? Was it last year, or the year before that?

I walk down the hall into the living area and notice that the light coming in through the windows of our little cabin looks bizarre. This small house in the woods sits up on a hill, and from the tall dining room picture windows I can see the tops of the huge pine and oak trees. It's a bit like being in a treehouse. But this view today isn't soothing. The house is glowing, a strange, creepy tint filtering in through the glass. I decide to walk outside to assess the smoke. As I look up through the tall cedar trees right off the deck, I know immediately that something is different, something is wrong. The skies are an unnatural glow of greens and oranges, and ash is collecting like deathly snowfall on the deck, on the cars, like an ominous dusting of the destruction that has begun. Andy follows me out onto the deck, looks up, and says, "We need to get out of here." I agree, and we go back in to grab a few essentials. This just got bumped up to code yellow or orange. Code yellowish orange.

We head back in, our earlier pace quickly evolving from cautionary to frantic. I am running through the house, spontaneously pulling a few pictures off the wall, when I realize Andy isn't in his room. He isn't gathering up any of his belongings. I call to him. "We need to pack up, Andy. Where are you?"

"In here."

I find him kneeling down in his little brother's room, packing up Tommy's things into a laundry basket. I see him grabbing Tommy's allowance, which is strewn about the room amidst the utter chaos that nine year olds seemingly thrive in. Andy then gets up and searches quickly for Froggie, Tommy's prized possession; a ragged stuffed animal that he sleeps with every night and plays with every day. Froggie is never far away from Tommy. Andy hurries into my room, flinging back the massive bed covers. He digs around and finds the frog buried under the pillows and tosses him in the laundry basket with some clothes for his little brother, a favorite Sponge Bob ball for stress, and random other items that Andy determines Tommy will need.

I stand frozen in place in awe, stunned that this kid who is the typical older brother is now acting in a way that is anything but typical. My kids fight. They yell, they torment, they annoy. Sometimes they even hit. They are brothers, and the age span has increased exponentially with Andy entering the early, heartbreaking stages of puberty. Suddenly the former best buds are now textbook older and younger siblings. So this act of kindness, of selflessness, doesn't escape my attention even during an evacuation.

I want to stay and watch this moment, let it stretch out for days and warm my heart. But I have to leave him there, and gather water, Motrin, and some snacks for the road. Just in case we hit some slow traffic, which isn't likely. We are leaving well ahead of the rush. We aren't even under an evacuation notice yet. We are getting out early. Just to be extra cautious and not take any chances. After reading about families that didn't make it out in time during the Carr wildfire in Redding, I'm not willing to stick around even for my most precious belongings. It isn't worth the risk to me, especially with a sick child.

I ask Andy if he can get our puppy, Harley, while I pack up the medicine and snacks. I hear him grab her harness and leash. "Walk her please," I call out to him through my rustling in the kitchen. Andy is sick today, but he is tough and will push through it. We have no choice right now anyway. The front door creaks open and I hear them head down the steps of the deck to the side yard. I head the other way across the deck, toward the car, and begin loading up my overnight bag, the laundry basket Andy packed up for Tommy, my purse, and our snack bag and water canteens. I am overwhelmed with that feeling you have when you are forgetting something but need to leave to get to work on time anyway. It's an ominous, deep feeling of wanting to stay to remember it all, to take it all with us.

As we try to load up the car, time speeds up to an abnormally fast pace. It's like time is passing us by, going on without us, and we are running to catch up to it. No matter how fast we drag out our bags to the car, it feels like we are not moving fast enough. I want more time, time to make sure I can get what we need, time to make sure we are grabbing the essentials. I just want more time, but there isn't any to spare. We leave most everything behind, because every minute spent packing could potentially delay our drive down the hill. It is so difficult to rush out of your home, your own space filled with so much love and memories, and not be able to take it all with you. Gut wrenchingly hard.

But in all honesty I do think we'll be returning, just like all the other times. I am at the very least hopeful and optimistic. An evacuation doesn't mean you can't go back later. It doesn't mean you lose all of your things. It doesn't mean your house will burn down. We have always been able to go back home. Every time. Either way, we don't have time to spare right now to pack up our treasures, our collections, our memories. As I walk out the door, a call comes through from reverse 911 to evacuate. I take a deep breath, take one last quick look at the living room and our unfinished game of chess, and lock up the handcrafted front door. Crossing the deck I glance up to see the wind chime that I made a few months earlier from the beautiful shells the boys and I collected at Point Reyes over the summer. *Damn.* No time to grab a ladder and get it, I think. It would take up too much time. There is just no time.

Chapter 2

For He shall give his angels charge over you to keep you in all your ways.

Psalm 91:11

9:14 a.m.

I am still standing on the deck and staring up at the wind chime when Andy runs up the stairs with Harley.

"Leave it," he says, knowing I am calculating how long it would take to get to the ladder. "Mom. We don't have time."

"I know, I just love those shells. We all collected those, remember?"

"Yeah, but we gotta go."

"Hopefully it's here when we get back." I turn and follow him across the deck and down to the car. From the driveway I see my neighbors packing up, loading up their car. I yell to them to hurry up and just get out.

"Be safe, love you!" They wave at us as we load up into the partially packed up car. I make a call to Ken, who is my ex-husband and the boys' father, to let him know that we are evacuating. We will head straight down to Chico. I should be there in plenty of time to pick up Tommy from school. Ken plans to be prepared to pick him up just in case, but we both agree that it's highly unlikely that the evacuation could take that long. They never take that long. I tell him I will call with an update if needed, if for any reason we are delayed. It is a routine evacuation call and backup plan, and neither of us is panicking. I disconnect and then call my cousin who is helping my grandmother and aunt. I alert them that there is a fire and that they need to get out. I hang up and glance back at Andy, knowing he is not feeling one hundred percent with this flu bug and a fever. His cheeks are still pink from the heat of it. "We got this, kiddo," I tell him.

"Yep." He nods at me, agreeing.

He's been through this before too. We all know the drill. Get the call, pack a bag, head down to a safer town. I slowly back out of the driveway, turning onto our street, clearing my mind of all that is being left behind. My focus has to be on getting us out of here, has to be in the present moment. And then we drive. We drive past the school, homes, the little store and gas station. We are eerily alone on the roads, seeing occasional people here and there packing up cars in their driveways with the trunks open. We wave, nod, and keep driving. No one looks panicked, just busy trying to save what they can. Many cars sit untouched, trunks closed, garage doors down, owners not visible. We do not pass any other vehicles for a few miles. When we get to the first stoplight, we finally see other cars, though most of them are not yet evacuating.

We drive toward the bridge and see thick oncoming traffic in the other lane. People are going back home to pack up and save what they can. Loved ones, pets, cherished items. I mention to Andy that it's good we are getting out now, ahead of the traffic. I explain how it's not worth it to wait or to try to save things. People's safety is the most important. Everything else can be left behind. He agrees. "At least we got Froggie," he says.

"Yes, Tommy will need him to sleep if we stay over somewhere."

We make it to the entrance of the bridge and I tell Andy, "This is good, we will be over the bridge in no time. Easy peasy." He nods, agreeing. And I think it is the truth. But I am so incredibly wrong.

As we slowly cross the bridge we look over to see that Sawmill Peak, a mountain within hiking distance away, is on fire. Not smoke, not ash, but actual fire. I slow down even more, my mouth gaping open in shock. How can this be? They only just put out the evacuation call. People will have no notice, no time to get out. There is a steady wind, which will push the fire. I begin to worry and I again call my cousin who is with my aunt and grandmother.

"Hey, are you on the road yet?"

"No, Grams is still gathering up stuff. You know how it is."

"Yeah, I know, but I'm at the bridge and Sawmill Peak is burning. You guys just need to go. Make her get in the car."

"Okay, will do. Call you in a bit from the road."

We finally cross the end of the bridge and what a relief it is to be over it during a disaster. I exhale long and slow, grateful to be on solid ground again. We round the first mountain curve off the bridge and the traffic is going up and around to the right on Old Skyway instead of straight down. Well, this is interesting. Why the detour already? It doesn't make sense. Maybe a fender bender? Maybe they are staging fire trucks? We turn right with the other traffic and slowly drive up the small and steep mountain road. We round a few bends, and then I am stunned at what I see. Burning houses, cars, trees. On fire. Actually on fire! We feel the heat permeate through the glass, heating the car. We keep driving. We just need to get out of here. We make it to the end of the road, with only several cars in front of us at the stop sign, all of us waiting to merge down onto Skyway at the Pentz road intersection. I look at Andy in the rearview mirror and say, "Get comfortable, here we go."

But we aren't going anywhere. We barely inch along. We finally make it past the stop sign and we just sit. So much time passes and we still aren't moving. My mind tries to make up for the lack of moving by running at the speed of light. My neurons fire back to back, a thousand thoughts crossing my mind in mere seconds. This isn't right. This hasn't happened before. Why aren't both lanes opened up to allow people out? Why aren't we moving even a little? There is still so far to go. We aren't even to Paradise yet. What are my options? This is not good. I look toward Pentz road and know that it's being closed. No one even tries to go in that direction. The fire must be near Pentz, maybe in the canyon. That leaves Clark road and Skyway as exit points. Two of the three exit paths. We just need to get further down Skyway. They will open up all four lanes to let people escape. Then traffic will begin to move.

But it doesn't move. And they don't open up all the lanes. I am getting stiff from sitting in the same position. By now we both desperately need to pee; it's been that long in the car. Hours already. It's smoky and the sun is a glowing red eye hanging in the sky like a sign of the Apocalypse. Still we aren't moving forward. I check the gas level and decide to cut the engine, even though we are in the Toyota. We sit in silence for a moment, just taking it all in and not believing it. It's been how long? Two hours? Three? Finally I tell Andy to leash the puppy, because we need to find a place to use as a bathroom area. He doesn't particularly like this idea, and neither do I, but sometimes in life you just don't get a choice.

We scope out the area, trying to assess what our options are. We are right in the middle of the intersection at Old Skyway and Pentz. To the left is a line of residential homes with a bike path and trees. To the right and up a steep slope sits a dilapidated commercial looking shop with no foliage. All around us are stopped cars full of other people, probably with the same thoughts and the same needs. I glance between the barren shop building and then back at the houses with landscaping and trees. To the left it is. We exit the car, lock it up, and walk toward the bike path and into some shrubs. There is not enough coverage so we try to block each other from the street side view. Andy goes first, I go second, and then we walk our puppy, Harley. There is still no sign of the cars moving even a little as we are walking back.

We get back into the car and just sit. We drink some water despite knowing that the side effect might be a challenge. I keep thinking, we have got to start moving. The traffic just needs to begin to move down the hill. And we are now! *Yes, hooray, thank you God!* We all begin to inch forward. We crawl forward about two car lengths and stop. Again. What is happening up there? Why are we still stuck? It is getting darker, smokier. The sun glows less. Everything is muted in an orange and green tinted fog. I notice big water droplets hitting the windshield, the windows, the hood. They splatter loudly onto the quiet car. *Snap, snap, snap.* I slide open the sunroof cover and we all look up and out through the wet glass. Choppers with huge buckets are looming overhead, probably filling up at Paradise Lake and the reservoir behind us. We watch them leave, both saddened and in awe of the sight. I am grateful they are here, but it's never a good sign. I send out a Facebook post with our status and the request for prayers. Something has to change.

We continue to sit and wait as the smoke gets thicker. Directly behind us is a huge Pepsi cargo truck, and behind that truck is one of my neighbors. Movement catches my eye and I watch as the Pepsi truck driver gets out of the truck, heads around to the back, and disconnects the trailer. Then he maneuvers the truck over off of the road and parks it, leaving the trailer directly in the middle of that intersection. Then the driver returns from the side of the road and begins unloading all of the cases of Pepsi, Gatorade, water. He brings water bottles to everyone in the nearby cars, and continues to unload crates and crates of drink, stacking one on top of another. This is so strange to me and Andy asks the same exact question that pops into my mind: why are they emptying out that trailer?

I continue to stare out the rearview mirror, with Andy looking out the back window, and it hits me. It hits my brain first, and then sinks down all the way into the pit of my stomach, where it hangs like a heavy lump of indigestible fear.

My throat tightens at the thought. They are going to put us in that. Andy turns back around, looks at me with questions all over his face, and I repeat my thought out loud. "They are going to put us in that." He blinks at me, and as I look at him after the truth has left my lips, it's my first real moment of terror. My stomach drops the rest of the way and I begin to shake. This is why we left early. This is why I never take any chances. This is exactly what I try to avoid with evacuations, what I try to avoid with my children. My mind balks at our current predicament. This just cannot be. A loud rap on the car window makes me jump. I turn around and look out of the water streaked glass. It's a local Sheriff, looking like this situation isn't in his manual. It isn't in mine either.

I roll down the window and he says, "The roads are currently blocked. If needed, we will all take shelter in that Pepsi truck, or along the side of it depending on the fire." I feel my head nodding, and I hear myself say to him, "Okay, I understand, thank you," as I roll up the window but in my head I'm saying there is No. Freaking. Way. No way! No. No a billion times over. How can this be the best option for all of these people? We will roast in that trailer. We will not survive in there. We can't all even fit into it. Do women and children still go first? How will it be determined who gets a spot? There has to be a better option. I look at Andy who is thinking the same exact thing. He shakes his head and says, "That is a terrible idea. Won't it be too smoky? Won't the container melt? It's going to get way too hot in that metal box." I nod, yes. Yes to all of those logical and rational thoughts during a crazy situation. I pray, and then I pray again. I pray for guidance, I pray for strength, I pray for help in the form of guardian angels, I pray for the hand of God and the Love of Jesus to be upon us and to wrap protectively around us. I pray for others, for safety and comfort. I pray for my sons, the brutally desperate and raw prayers of a mother's love and hopes and dreams.

Chapter 3

Do not be afraid, for I am with you.

Isaiah 41:10

When I open my eyes from prayer I see that Andy is visibly shaking.

"How are you doing, Andy?" I ask, scanning his face. "You're shaking," I tell him.

"I think I am n-n-nervous or c-c-cold" he manages, teeth chattering, voice calm.

"Yeah, me too kiddo," and I hold up my hand as it quivers from adrenaline. And I think, he is like me. *Just like Mommy.* He is scared, and understands the threat, but he is calm. I see his mind working trying to figure this puzzle out, trying to problem solve. I think back to him as a baby, before he could even speak, how he would inspect toys. Give him a car and he'd immediately turn it over to see how it worked. Years later he would work on mazes and any puzzles he could find. And now, an accomplished young master of Rubik's cubes and developer of algorithms. There is no algorithm for this. No scientific, proven set of rules to follow that will solve this problem. But that doesn't stop the mind from trying. My mind is spinning it out too. Should I just cut over and drive down in the wrong lane? How far could we get? What is going on that has traffic so backed up? What will we do if they tell us to get inside that Pepsi truck? To load up my kid and dog in what is basically going to be an oversized roasting box? To agree to an imminent death? I honestly don't think I can do that.

People are getting outside of their parked cars now, looking panicked, talking to the Sheriff, talking to each other. Some share cigarettes, some share water. Some walk their dogs. Some walk down toward our "bathroom" area amidst the sparse foliage. I watch them through the windows and windshield and I know we are all trying to wrap our minds around this being our reality, and it isn't working for any of us. All of our faces show raw emotions; so much that people only make eye contact for a brief knowing moment and then look away. As if it's too painful and real and horrifying to empathize right now. Or maybe they are searching for answers but don't find any. Looks of confusion, frustration, fear. People point to Pentz road. Heads shake. No, it's not open. No traffic through. People leave their cars and go talk to the Sheriff. Those chats aren't going well either.

Calls are being made on cell phones, with frantic updates to loved ones. I imagine the conversations that everyone is having are all very similar. *What is the fire status? Do you have any information on the road conditions? Get out if you haven't left yet. We didn't have time to grab anything. We are still stuck here at Pentz road. Why isn't the traffic moving? It's really smoky and they want to stick us in a metal Pepsi box. This is so insane. Pray for us. I love you.*

Another knock at the window pulls my thoughts back and I again roll it down. The Sheriff clears his throat, probably a side effect from the smoke, or from nerves. "Traffic will begin to move soon. You will drive down toward Clark road." All I can do is nod. I'm too numb to feel relieved yet. Somebody somewhere just made a good judgment call to try and get us out of here. People hurriedly return to their vehicles and all of the cars behind the Pepsi truck are getting routed back up into Magalia, and those in front of it down into Paradise. My neighbor makes a sharp U-turn, and heads back up into the mountains. I wave and pray for her as the car slowly disappears around the bend. We creep forward further down into Paradise, a false sense of security in place thinking there is a plan and thinking that we will get out. I watch the Pepsi trailer, slowly shrinking in the back window. Finally I can no longer see it, the imminent death trap mercifully out of view. It takes us another half an hour to move less than a mile. Inch forward, stop. Inch forward, stop. *Inch, inch, inch.* We begin to move a little faster, 3 mph, 5 mph, 7, 8, 9. Andy has to pee again but there is nowhere to pull over, no shoulder at all, and we can't just stop in the road. He is desperate. I hand him a plastic container I keep in the car door for trash.

"Seriously?" he asks, clearly understanding the gravity of our situation and peering into the container as if it might reveal an answer of sorts like a magic eight ball. *Yes, no, most likely, it is decidedly so, ask again later.* It reveals nothing.

"You have two choices kiddo. Go or don't."

"I have to."

"Then do it. I know this sucks but you just do it anyway. You got this."

He nods, resigned, somehow managing to pee into the container (I don't ask) and I know he's thinking that things just got real. He looks at me, looks at the full container, and back at me. Now we have a different problem to address.

"We are moving really slow. Open your door and pour it out the best you can." I slow the car down even more, and he manages to open the door to pour it out and shuts the door, then hands me the empty container. I take it, but seriously, how is this our life right now? I prop it upright on the floor of the passenger side foot area. We drive until traffic backs up again. Inch forward, *inch, inch, inch.* How much time passes? I've quit tracking it at this point. And again we stop. I try to make a call out to let family know an update. No cell service. Is it just where we are on this little mountain road? Or are the cell towers gone already? Typically I do have a couple of bars in this area, as it's close enough to town to get reception. That I can't get a call out isn't a good sign.

We creep to a stop. Why are we stopped again? We wait and wait. I cut the engine again to conserve fuel. I look around us. It's mostly residential, a small two lane road, with still only one lane of traffic open for evacuation. This doesn't seem right. So many people are trying to get out and there is still only one lane open? A random guy knocks on the car window. "They might send us out on foot. If you have to get out and run, bring something to cover your face. Don't wet it down." I'm not sure if I say anything or not. I think my mouth hangs open, jaw slack. He moves on and I roll up the window. Stressful situations make people do crazy things. Get out of the car? Yeah, right. My mind rejects the concept immediately. We sit and wait.

    A police vehicle creeps up behind us and uses the oncoming traffic lane to cruise by us all. I crane my neck around and maneuver the car as far to the left as I can, trying to see if there is a narrow path we can take and follow the cop car. I catch Andy watching me closely in the rearview mirror. "Mom, are you going rogue?" Wow, my kid knows me. Knows my brain. Knows I will do whatever it takes to get us out of this. Knows I am thinking of following that police car down the hill until we get out of traffic or get arrested. Either way would be fine.

    "I'm not sure, Andy. I don't know what's down there. Not sure how far we'd get. I need a minute to think this through." I continue to consider the idea. My body screams at me to go! Go! Just pull the car over and barrel through the other lane, up onto the dirt if necessary. There hasn't been any oncoming traffic at all. It's very, very tempting to get out of line and make our own way. This is the epitome of the fight or flight response at its finest. I think back to last year and grad school, to the training for crisis response in a disaster. The first responders know things that we don't. Hopefully their communications are still functioning. They have a bigger picture. They are trained for these situations. We need to do what they tell us to do, even if it sounds insane. Even if it actually is insane.

We wait some more, and I explain the reasons why to Andy. Panicked actions, panicked people, will not help a situation like this. If I come completely unhinged and begin driving up the side of the road, it may lead others to do that as well. We have no way of knowing what is up ahead, but if cars can't get through it's likely not good.

We continue to sit in silence until we hear the crackle of a loudspeaker and a booming voice broadcasting out of it. "If the fire gets too close, get out of your cars and start moving South toward Clark road." Get out and go on foot? What the hell is happening? My mind half laughs, half yells, no, NO, not going to happen. That is crazy talk. *Cray cray*. They need to open up all lanes of Skyway and get us all out of here. Right now. Open up the lanes. Get us out.

Just in case, or maybe for something to do, I grab the Swiss Army backpack I use for work. Andy had grabbed it and thrown it in the car without me even knowing. What a rock star. I unzip it and dump out my folders, along with my laptop and charger. Those typically protected, valuable items just got bumped to the bottom of the priority list. Survival items are now bumped up to the top. Where we might possibly go on foot, I have no idea. There has to be water at the bottom of the canyon. And with it bears and mountain lions. That hike would take hours and hours. But I pack up anyway. Into my backpack go water canteens, Motrin, the snack bag, my cell phone. Ironically, I completely forget about the first aid kit and hand warmers in the glove box in case of…yeah…emergency. I glance into the backseat and Andy is sitting there, stunned and frozen.

"Andy, pack a bag." My kids and I like to hike. We travel. They know what it means to pack a bag. They know some survival basics. Take only the necessities. Choose wisely what you pack on your body. Plan ahead, be aware, take water, layer clothing, no horsing around. Only they haven't had to do it in an emergency. Andy figures it out quickly though, mimicking me and dumping out his Chromebook and whatever else he doesn't need from his backpack. He grabs a couple of baby blankets we use in the car for the dog, grabs her little jacket, his hoodie, her baggie of dog food. I hear him clipping on her leash. I hear the blood pressure fill my ears and squeeze my head.

Andy starts in with the questions. "Do we have to get out? Where would we go? Will Harley be okay on foot? Can we just carry her? Why can't we get through with the car?"

My mind is asking the same questions, and in this moment, I just don't have any of the answers. Where would I possibly lead them? In an earthquake, to a doorway or outside clearing. In a tornado, the innermost lower section of a building or in a ravine, abandoning the vehicle. In a tsunami, to the highest ground possible. But wildfire? I know what to do in a house fire, but a wildfire? I am not prepared to run on foot from a wildfire. I continue to try and problem solve. There are no bodies of water near us at this location, probably not even any residential pools.

Before I can formulate a response to my child, a loudspeaker crackles and snaps again. "Prepare to exit your vehicles and head on foot toward Clark road. The fire is too close. Abandon your vehicles and move South toward Clark road." At this point utter chaos ensues. People fling open their car doors, looking around with wild expressions, yelling, and begin to move. Car doors are left ajar and people move down the street as fast as they can. I don't realize I've been holding my breath until I let it out, slow and deliberate. How can it be safer to get out of the car? I turn and look at Andy, who is thinking the same thing. Something behind him catches my eye. Bright orange. Up in the pine trees. "Oh no. God, no, no, no." This can't be. I cover my mouth with my hands but don't need to as I have no other words. No sound or air escapes my throat. I just stare. Andy is asking me muffled questions that blur into the background but I can't answer. Finally I point, and he turns and looks out the side window, then looks up. Way up. He sees what I see, and then slowly turns his head around and looks back at me. His face pales, the flush of his fever wiped from his cheeks. His wide, dark hazel eyes get even darker, the pupils dilating huge and black, taking over the green and brown. I know this look. It's the look of terror.

Chapter 4

'And I myself will be a wall of fire around her,' declares the Lord, 'and I will be the glory in the midst of her.'

Zechariah 2:5

1:30 p.m.

The next time you walk past a huge pine tree or redwood, look up at the top of it, up to the sky. Lean way back, stretch your neck up so you can see all the way to the very top like young children do when looking at trees. Imagine at least the top half of it on fire. Then visualize all of the other tall trees next to that one, for miles and miles, and they are all on fire too. Envision hill after hill, mountain after mountain, town after town, all on fire. Picture an unfathomable wall of flames stretching into the sky, Hell itself trying to reach into Heaven. Now imagine that between that tidal wave of fire and where you are sits your child, looking at you, eyes wide and expectant.

    I quickly check my cell phone. Still no service. It has to be that the cell towers are gone. I send out the following messages via Facebook Messenger, to a colleague that I know will be checking and able to help. I don't send any messages out to my family at this point because they are all evacuating too and likely won't check Messenger if they even have it. I send the last message with the time included because I have no idea when it will actually be delivered, or if at all, followed by a photo to show where we are with the hope that we won't need Search and Rescue to find us.

    Me: Call my ex-husband tell him we are on foot but okay 530-XXX-XXXX have him call my mom

Me: If you get these it's 1:39 right now

Me: [Uploaded photo of the fire right by the street]

They are the last messages that I will send out for hours and hours. I do not yet know how bad things are about to get, or that I will not be able to get any more messages out to anyone. Not to my mom. Not to the boys' father. Not to my sweet, sweet Tommy. No I love yous. No goodbyes. I don't have time to think about this until it is too late.

I look around us again, look for any way possible to put us in a better place. Where we are parked is not good. We are right in the middle of this narrow mountain road, with other vehicles around us for as far as the eye can see. Huge trees line the road on both sides, and low power lines loom overhead. I pull the car over to the right, slowly maneuvering around all the abandoned cars and trucks, and drive on the shoulder just far enough to put a little more distance between us and the fire. I don't have all wheel drive, but the Highlander is up off the ground enough to drive over a curb, debris, and heavy enough to balance us on the slope of the shoulder. Even if we get the vehicle stuck, it's worth the risk.

I see a decent spot to park and pull off the road into a small storage unit driveway. It's not big, but it's fairly clear of trees, and it's better than parking on the street by all the trees and utility lines. I throw the car into park and tell Andy to get out. We load up with the backpacks, my camera, and the puppy, heading South as instructed toward Clark road, and the Fastrip Gas Station. Yes, directly toward a gas station. *Oy vey*. The fire snaps and crackles loudly, the sound of a bonfire times a billion. Sparks, ash, debris, and huge, demonic flames are right there behind us. They don't dance or flicker. They eat everything. A home right across the street is burning to the ground, completely destroyed. How is this happening? How are all of my maternal efforts to be extra cautious failing us? I can't wrap my brain around it.

We finally make it down to Clark road, and I do not like the look of it. We pause at a what I hope is a safe distance from the gas station as I assess what is ahead of us. It is all residential, wooded areas. I can't think of a place that can provide shelter, they are all too far away on foot. We are told to keep going, but I keep us there, knowing we can't go that way. The heated wind whips my hair and flushes my face.

Most of the people continue down Clark only for emergency personnel to turn everyone around. Now we have to back track our steps. We head back up the hill, back toward the gas station. I look to the left. We can't go that way now, it's all blocked and burning. I look to the right and see trees on fire there too. We can't go that way either. I stand in the middle of the road and turn in a slow, complete circle shaking my head at each blocked route. *Nope, nope, nope*. People are panicking, frantically looking around, not knowing what to do. I don't hear the sound of their screams, it is all blocked out. Some people try to run, though I don't know how far they can go. My guess is: not very far. I keep us near to the road, unwilling to get too much closer to the gas station.

I'm confused as to how we are completely surrounded on all four sides, because typically in an evacuation we know where the fire is at and we know which direction it is headed. This fire is a foreign creature because the winds are blasting so hard that the fire and sparks literally get shot out all around us, creating spot fires that then grow and merge into one huge beast that engulfs everything in a three hundred sixty degree radius around us. It is definitive; we are trapped.

Chapter 5

In all your ways acknowledge Him, And He shall direct your paths.

Proverbs 3:6

A loud, booming voice yells, "Everyone! Get over here!" It is a firefighter, his reflective stripes and helmet number gleaming in the firelight. He keeps calling and waving his arms as we all call out to others further away and follow him to a newly poured, small cement slab that is framed by three little buildings still under construction. Crazed and terrified people keep filing in from all directions, gathering in close to one another, elbows nearly touching. It looks to be about one hundred people, maybe more, all crowding onto the slab with their bags and pets and prayers. The firefighter begins to speak again.

"Okay, listen up. There is no way out. All of the roads are blocked. Power lines are down, trees are down, cars are blocking the way. We have no way to get out in any direction. It is not safe on foot. Stay calm and listen to the instructions so we can keep everyone safe." People immediately begin to panic at the instructions to stay calm. They begin to talk amongst themselves, some begin to cry, some to shout questions at the first responders.

"Open up Skyway!"

"We will all die here!"

"Call for help!" The chatter is getting louder and louder. My mind begins to block out the sound of everything except the blood rushing through my ears. The yelling, the sobbing, the hissing of the fire. It all fades away, making room in my mind to try and grasp what is happening. The thought of no way out with my child permeates my brain first, and then travels to the rest of my body in a slow, cold, ugly way. *Fear*. I look around us. Thick smoke, ash, debris, and flames are getting closer, from all sides. How can we literally be surrounded by fire in this tiny little space? I keep hearing the firefighter's words in my mind on instant replay. No. Way. Out.

The firefighter's voice calls out again. "This is what is going to happen. You will lie down on the cement, staying as low as possible. You will cover your faces with whatever you have. Keep your bodies positioned to brace for impact. If the choppers need to drop buckets of water on us to keep us alive they will. They know where we are. The water will hit you hard so keep your heads low and prepared. The fire is going to blow right over us. The winds are strong and it is moving fast. Stay calm and do not panic. If you follow these instructions we should all get out of here."

At this point I'm pretty sure they are trained to say this last bit just to help control panicked crowds of people in a disaster. Because it honestly doesn't look at all like any of us are getting out alive. It looks like walls of fire are surrounding us and there is nowhere to go, nothing to do about it. It looks like the end of time. I wrap my cell phone in a plastic baggie and zip it closed. I stuff it into the middle of my backpack, which is durable but probably isn't waterproofed. Maybe the phone will survive in there if water is dumped on us. Maybe it will survive even if we don't; the pictures of this day telling authorities the thousands of words I want to be mine. The words for my family, for Tommy. There is still so much to teach, to show, to love. I'm not done yet.

Cars begin to melt from the radiant heat all around us. Actual cars are being taken over by this monster incinerator of a wildfire. Truck bumpers begin to droop from the intense heat, looking like Dali's painted clock in *Persistence of Memory*.

Brake lights drip, rivulets of paint and plastic and aluminum bleeding onto the road and pooling like candle wax. These scars forming on the pavement will likely remain for years and years. How does one remove melted vehicle materials that have bonded to the asphalt? The fire burns at a horrific three thousand degrees Fahrenheit, over double the temperature of a typical wildfire. Because of this, towns are being completely flattened. I think of the movie *Apocalypse Now*, and the orders given to "terminate with extreme prejudice." There will be nothing to find even in the ashes. Nothing to sift through, nothing to salvage. It's all just turning to dust right before our eyes.

  How do scientists measure wildfires? I'm pretty certain as of yet there is no scale to determine how powerful a fire is. Everything else has a form of measurement or assessment. Gale force winds have knots or miles per hour, tornadoes the Fujita scale, even tsunamis have an acoustic signaling tool that transmits height measurements to satellites which help to predict its progress. Earthquakes, hurricanes, and volcanoes also have scales used to determine strength, amplitude, power. Where does this fire fall on a hypothetical measurement scale? It's got to be whatever the highest numeric recording value is going to be if one is ever invented. This wildfire is a beast. A living, breathing entity; sucking up all of our oxygen and leaving us choking on carbon dioxide and gasping for air.

  Incandescent particles flit about with long, thin, orange glowing trails. I watch as these sparks flicker into lethal little fireflies, which then metamorphose into even deadlier Chinese dragons, arching and swirling, burning. They eventually all become one. This fire has many heads, many mouths with tongues flicking out, offering the kiss of death.

  We lie down on the cement. People's bodies are bumped up against strangers, the space is that small. I gather Andy and Harley close to me and try to position Andy's head, cushioning and protecting it with my body. He is using the tiny dog coat to cover his face, with the little hood fitting over his mouth and nose like a breathing mask. I cover my face by folding a loose weave sweater for work that I found in the backseat of the car. Not ideal, but better than nothing. I wrap all of our heads with the baby blankets the best that I can, tucking them in around our necks until most of the light is blocked out. All I can do is make this as comforting as possible for my child. I can't save Andy, can't save us. I remember a church that we pass every day on our drive that always has messages on the sign by the road. It currently reads: *You can't. God can*. I breathe in the smoky air. I accept what I cannot do. I pray for what God can do.

We lay like this for hours, my body beginning to ache from being in the same position on a concrete slab under an eighty pound kid and a fifteen pound puppy. We try not to shift, because the small blankets only just cover our faces. Time seemingly crawls, the space time continuum warped and stretched by impending doom, or being isolated under a blanket, or from the searing heat and smoke of hellfire. Eons pass and Andy then reminds me that drinking water helps our bodies filter out the smoke. He continues to tell me every eon or two to hydrate.

"Do you have your canteen?" And, "Drink water." "Time to have some water." I do as he says because I don't have the heart to tell him that we aren't likely making it out of this. It's too violent, too gruesome, too powerful. I can't see any way out for us. But I say none of this.

Instead of speaking, we constantly sip on our water. Finally he tells me he has to pee. It surprises me that he didn't tell me sooner. It can't wait any longer, he is nearly in pain from having to go. I prop up on an elbow and look around. There is nowhere to go and we have to stay low. We are lying next to a parking curb filled with dirt that is likely intended to hold a few shrubs or small trees after construction of the area is complete. It's either the dirt or the pavement, and at least the dirt will provide drainage and containment.

But that only solves part of the problem. We are surrounded by a huge crowd of other people. My mind hunts and I pull up an old conversation with one of the Little League coaches describing how males can discreetly urinate when needed. I explain the process to Andy, "Here is what you need to do. Take a knee, down close to the dirt. Reach up under the leg of your shorts for access and do your best." He looks at me incredulously, and around at all of the people huddling together in close proximity. "Buddy, I know this is crazy. This is what happens in emergency situations. You are not alone with this. Now is not the time to care about what people think or what they might see. Heads are covered and no one is even going to notice. Now do it quickly and try to hold your breath because your face won't be covered." He nods once, takes a breath, drops the jacket from his face, and kneels down. We are here for so long that this process is repeated a few more times. Huddle for hours, get up to pee. *Huddle, pee, repeat.*

Someone walks around, inviting people to pray. I hear his voice muffled through our blankets saying, "Anyone that wants to pray is welcome. Come and sit with us if you like. If you can't, don't worry, we will be praying for you." I want to get up, but have Andy and Harley tucked in tight and we are all so sleepy from the smoke. So exhausted. I raise my arm up and wave my hand, keeping it up, hoping he sees it and knows it is a sign. *Yes, please, pray for us. For this child and for my other child. For all of us. For everyone. Please pray.*

We continue to lie there, and the air is getting dark and cold, similar to a full eclipse. Another apocalyptic sign. Our world goes black and freezing even though it is on fire. We are cold but too drugged from the smoke to shiver. Andy is in shorts and slipper socks, because he didn't worry about himself when he was packing up Tommy's things. I look down at the green and white striped fuzzy socks and goose bumps all over his legs. Probably from the cold air, and probably from his fever. We should be home in bed cuddling. We should be home resting. We should be with Tommy, home from school by now. Instead we are under the tiny dog blanket, Harley falling asleep on my legs. Andy checks on her constantly. Is she breathing? Is she okay? He nudges her to make sure she is still conscious, still alive. I cough and choke and gag on the smoke, it is that thick. I manage through sheer will to not vomit, but my body is trying to reject this much smoke regardless of what I want. This is all just so wrong. And it's about to get worse.

Through the blanket we hear the firefighter voice booming out at us again. "Okay, listen up folks. The fire is approaching. It's blowing at over eighty miles an hour. It's going to blast through here. It's going to get hot, it's going to get smoky. Stay down and keep your faces covered." Does he mean hotter than it was before? Does he mean smokier? I can't imagine more smoke is even possible. We do as he says, waiting for it to hit. I hear it before I feel it. The shrieking roar of the wind and the sound of everything burning. Trees, cars, homes, and worse. The sound is a firestorm, with crackling, popping, roaring, and the scream of a banshee wind howling around us. It is loud and steady, a burning freight train through Hell. The wind velocity is so powerful that a vortex of fire is created, sickly twisting up into the sky. The fire actually creates its own unique weather system which is a terrifying concept. We hear buildings fall in on themselves, trees crash to the ground. People scream, people cry, people sob.

"We're going to die," a woman wails nearby, and I think she is right. Someone sobs out "I love you babe." Someone wails. Someone chants. Someone hyperventilates. Someone is singing, a soft, lilting voice carrying through the waves of demonic winds. I pull Andy and Harley so tightly against me I have to make sure I don't suffocate us before the smoke does. And then the explosions begin.

Chapter 6

The Lord is close to all who call on Him.

Psalm 145:18

It turns out that the cement lot we are on is situated next to a propane tank storage field. As the fire takes over, they begin to blow. Each time one detonates the air reverberates around us, hitting our chests, and the ground shakes like earthquake tremors. They explode so often it sounds and feels like bombs are going off. In reality, they are. "It's a freaking war zone!" a man yells. His voice is raspy with a touch of hysteria. My heart goes out to him; he is likely a veteran and it does look and sound just as he describes. It is a war zone, and we are completely surrounded by the enemy. I can hear the panic in his voice.

    I have a soft spot in my heart for Vets. Most of my graduate study research included Veterans and PTSD. I used every chance I had to learn more about techniques that could help this population. Twenty two veterans commit suicide each day. The statistics are staggering. These are our heroes, our defenders. The veterans in my family include my Gramps, several Uncles, Cousins, and Dad. My father is a Veteran from the Vietnam War. His purple heart is in my car right now. *I'm glad you're not here to experience this Papa. Sorry we won't be trading stories.*

    As we huddle tighter, I can't stop thinking about how we are right across the street from the gas station. This is not going to be good. The cold air moves out and it starts to get hot. The howling wind brings with it a blasting heat, like when you open an oven or use a blow dryer, only exponentially worse. The cold that fell around us before gets pushed away by gale force flaming winds. Now when we shake we know it is not from the cold, it is from the fear. Huge red orange embers fall with the ash and debris. It's so hot and so smoky and all around us is just…fire. Everything in a full radius around this lot is being decimated. No way are any of us making it out of here alive. How one single day, one shift of the wind, one illness with a fever, one Thursday, can change everything, is mind boggling. This is not how it is supposed to go, I think, but yet it is. *This is.*

"Love you Andy."

"Love you."

I take his hand in mine, so heartbroken that I can't protect him. I feel so incredibly sad that Tommy is going to lose his mom and older brother and puppy all at the same time. Feeling like I failed them. It's the worst feeling I've ever experienced. We are going to asphyxiate, if we are lucky. I envision the ruins I saw in Pompeii, a mother cradling her child in her arms, frozen in ash. Andy and I are in the same position, feeling sleepy from the smoke. Harley's breathing isn't good, and I hate that she will go first, that Andy will have to see it. My heart breaks for him, splits right in two. One half for Andy, the other half for Tommy. My sweet boys.

As I hold Andy, I think about how great he makes my life. He is my hero that gets the car door for me every morning before we drive to school. My hero that makes the best cheesy pasta and quesadillas. My hero that tutors his little brother with homework on days that I am ill. My hero that never, ever complains. My hero that walks the dog every day. Does the dishes, makes me laugh, pranks us constantly. My. Hero. Always.

"I'm so glad Tommy isn't here for this," Andy quietly shares.

"Me too. And I'm so sorry you are. I'm so, so sorry, baby." Sorry that I can't save him. Sorry that I won't be here to help him and Tommy. Won't be here to become a counselor.

Won't be here to help people that need help. Sorry that my family will lose us. They will all be left behind to grieve. My other son. My mom. My brother. My dad. My grandmother. If she got out. She was with my cousin and auntie. I pray they got out.

I pull Andy closer to me and hold him. Without saying anything, I tuck him into me and begin the Lord's Prayer out loud. He immediately begins to pray it with me, our voices muffled under the blanket and the wind and the fire. The Devil himself is trying to blot out the sound. *But God hears us anyway.*

"Our Father, who art in Heaven, hallowed be Thy name. Thy kingdom come, Thy will be done, on Earth as it is in Heaven. Give us this day our daily bread, and forgive us our trespasses as we forgive those who trespass against us. And lead us not into temptation, but deliver us from evil. For Thine is the Kingdom, the Power, and the Glory forever. Amen."

Then we wait, drowsy and exhausted, unable to filter out all of the smoke as we breathe. At this point I have no idea of how many hours have passed, but it feels like a lifetime. Like I have aged a million years in a day. Like there is no time, only the waiting for it to end. The waiting is stretching out and time no longer exists, as if we are being pulled nearer to the center of a black hole and the gravitational force stops light, time, everything.

We don't fall asleep, though many do. We just get drowsy and our bodies sink down heavy on the cement. There comes a point where I don't think, I don't speak, I don't even pray. I have said it all and have made my peace. I believe Andy has too. We cling to each other not out of desperation but out of love. He relaxes against me and I am no longer afraid, no longer sad, no longer resisting the inevitable.

Eventually, after timeless hours have passed, I have to change my body position. I can't feel my left leg at all. It is numb all the way up to my lower back. I can't even move it.

We have laid here so long that my limb doesn't even respond to my mind trying to shift it. I gently move Andy off me and try to drag my leg by the seam of my pants into a different position. I finally manage rolling to the side and sitting upright. I scoot backwards a bit hoping it will allow circulation to my leg. And in doing so I uncover our heads and see that the embers all around us are huge, luminescent and dancing through the sky, floating down around us. Deadly little lanterns. They land and form globules on the cement, emitting glowing red orange light. One lands on a woman nearby and her jacket catches on fire. Oh no, not this. Now people are catching on fire. Someone beats on her coat and puts it out. I stare in horror, unable to move or speak or think or feel.

I am about to cover us up with the blanket again, which will either be for protection or ignition, when I see a huge firefighter with an equally huge axe begin to cross the lot with a vengeance. He holds the axe at an angle across his massive chest, with one hand near the axe head and the other hand lower on the handle. Because time has stopped, he moves in slow motion, pushing through whatever inexplicable pull has paused the four fundamental forces of the universe. He walks in full strides like a warrior going into battle, in his full suit of golden armor and ancient weapon in hand. Whatever is about to happen, I need to see it and can't look away.

Chapter 7

Together they will be like warriors in battle trampling their enemy into the mud of the streets. They will fight because the LORD is with them, and they will put the enemy horsemen to shame.

Zechariah 10:5

On the lot's perimeter stand three small new buildings, still not completed. The closest one to us is going to be, was going to be, a crepe shop. The buildings are little, but are built of all new construction materials, and are commercial properties with metal roofing. The firefighter warrior walks right up to the glass door of the closest building, raises the axe, and swings it into the glass. It shatters and cracks and spills onto the cement. Swing, crash. Swing, crash. He busts out all of the glass left within the metal framing of the doors. Crash, crash, crash. We stare in awe. It's a powerful sight. He stands there with his huge boots in a pile of shimmering safety glass, axe at his side, assessing the inside of the building. It is one of the most badass things I've ever seen in person.

People murmur in hushed amazement and slowly get up; we move a bit closer to the building to find out what is going to happen next. The fire crew gathers us around with their plan to try and keep us alive. We will seek shelter in the first building. When it catches on fire, we will rotate over to the second building, and then to the third, moving when the fire determines that we must move. Staying indoors will help to lessen the threat of people catching on fire. The fire crew enters the building and conducts a swift safety check. When they reappear out on the lot, they give us all the go ahead to move inside.

We shuffle in and set up a space, apparently waiting for the building to ignite at some point. The floor is concrete so we put down one blanket and use the other as cover. We wait, and then wait some more, for how many hours I cannot say. Live embers flitter into the building. Andy stomps out a larger one that lands on the floor. We are low on water, and what is left of the sun through the smoke begins to fade as it sets. It's going to get cold tonight.

Andy asks, "Are we going to camp here overnight?"

"That's a good question. I'm not sure." Not if the building burns down we won't. Not if we die from smoke. We could certainly use more supplies than what we have on us to get through the night. If we make it that long. I stand up, stretch, and carefully walk to the shattered glass door area and look out. Everything is still on fire. I step outside and look around further. I watch a firefighter using a shovel and dirt to fight the flames closest to us. I stare at the little burning patches just feet from our building. There must be twenty live spots just in this small section. The shovel cuts into the ground, grabs a pile of dirt, and suffocates a tiny fire spot. Scoop, dump. Scoop, dump. Scoop, scoop, dump. I observe the firefighter and I am either mesmerized or in shock, or both. As I watch the shovel scrape and dig, it doesn't hit me yet that there are no hoses being used, no tankers parked nearby. *No water.*

The gas station across the street is still under extreme threat. The home right next door to its parking lot is burning. All of the surrounding trees are burning. The outlook doesn't look good. What happens if that station blows? It's so close to us. What type of explosion does that create? I look around me at all the people, all the dogs. We have all been here so long, for hours and hours. If we do survive the fire, we are going to need water soon. Survival law: shelter first, then water, then food. I consider our options. If we get desperate enough someone could raid the gas station food for food and water, but right now that is likely the last resort. I make up my mind and go back into the building to tell Andy the plan. I have to get back to the car.

Andy and Harley sit on the blanket, huddled together. Andy's face is flushed, eyes glassy. I place my face to his cheek, then I gently touch the back of my hand to his forehead. He's burning up. My mommy thermometer registers him at about 102. We run the risk that it could spike in the night. I dig through my backpack.

"Motrin time kiddo."

"Okay."

"I didn't pack anything to mix it with, sorry. I thought we would be down in Chico way before now. It's not going to taste great, so just sip some Motrin and then take a drink of water. Motrin, water, Motrin, water. Do that until it's gone."

He does, and I know it must taste bad because the smell alone is pretty awful. Like cherry flavored bile. But he doesn't complain. He hasn't complained once through this entire ordeal. Sick, feverish, and terrified, but not complaining. God, I love this child so much. Thank you God that...I can't even finish the thought. It's too much. I'm so grateful, yet right now my gratitude is complicated by other, bittersweet emotions.

The smoke is not as thick in this little building, but we also can't close off that broken doorway, so it is just a matter of time until it rolls in to choke us. We sit in silence, until I can't take it any longer. I lean over to Andy and start to quietly sing an old Tom Petty song at a low volume, just for our ears.

"You don't have to live like a refugee (don't have to live like a refugee) No you don't..." He interrupts me, "Mom. Seriously?" but he is smiling.

'How about Pink?' I sing, "Just like fire, burning out the way..."

Andy actually laughs. "I had no idea you were this sick."

"Yeah, I know. I could keep going."

He chuckles and says, "Nah, I'm good."

We smile at each other, grateful that the comic relief moment boosted our spirits even just a little. People eventually begin to walk around as the falling debris seems to be less threatening. Andy's face seems less flushed. Fire all around us outside, and Andy is burning off some virus on the inside. The threat of heat is everywhere right now, mocking our attempt at survival. But the Motrin is working, and so are the prayers.

We decide to walk the dog and Andy wants to check out the second building that has just been busted open. We leave our packs and blankets propped up against the unfinished wall, briefly stretch our stiff bodies, and cautiously move out of Building One and into the fire zone. It still looks like Hell outside. We walk across the small cement slab to Building Two, and a few people are inside it already, setting up their makeshift camp area. I wait outside and let Andy scope it out on his own. He comes back out, shaking his head. "The floor isn't finished yet, it's rough gravel still. Harley would be too uncomfortable on that."

"Okay, we can stay in Building One until it's no longer safe."

We both have to pee, again. We walk around the backside of Building Two. There is a cement retaining wall which has likely offered some protection from the flames. Past it there are trees still burning, and piles of red coals spotted all around for as far as we can see. Against the back of the building there are multiple wet spots along the sidewalk where others have figured out that there is nowhere else to go. It's fairly private, considering the circumstances. I go first, then Andy. We walk the dog back along what will probably be a parking area, but it's still dirt for now. The puppy finally goes, and I use a baggie from her leash dispenser to clean it up, looking around for a garbage.

"You know, today, you could probably just leave that," Andy comments, gesturing out at the mass destruction all around us. But for some reason we still go through the motions of normalcy, even when this is anything but normal. I find a small dumpster nearby that was left here for the construction crew and toss the bag in, wishing I could wash my hands. But we have bigger things to worry about. I need to take this time to bring up my plan for the night, so I turn to my son as we walk back and into the building.

"Andy, we all need water. And if we end up staying overnight it's going to be really cold. There are more supplies in the car."

"No."

"Look, I am going to leave you and Harley here in Building One with everyone. I will hike back to the car, grab some stuff, and come right back. The threat is much less than earlier."

"No."

"Andy, honey, I have to go try."

He sees it in my eyes. The determination. The stubbornness. The decision is already made. I'm not asking for his input on this one. I know he doesn't like it, and I don't either. But I am going to do it anyway. Andy continues to have a silent staring contest with me. Finally, he exhales slowly, and sits down by our packs with the dog, breaking eye contact and staring straight ahead with his face passive.

"I will be right back."

"Yep."

I kiss him and walk out of the building, out into the ruins.

Chapter 8

You don't understand now what I am doing, but someday you will.

John 13:7

Yesterday, I found that my new water distiller had stopped working. Irritated, I drove to the store, and bought five gallons of bottled water. It is still in the back of my car, not making the priority list of things that got done yesterday. The water is a big reason to make the hike back to the car. There are more blankets in there too, and some clothes. A first aid kit is in the glove box along with some pocket hand warmers. I always have a small collection of various items stored in the car in case of emergency, even if I don't remember that they are there during said emergency.

I cross the lot and step over the curb, hiking through all the construction dirt piled up alongside the road. Abandoned vehicles stretch for as far as I can see in both directions. Small burn piles are all that are left of homes, garages, and sheds. Trees are gone or are smoldering, a few still burning. Bright orange sparks flit about the air. The smoke and ash are still thick, making the air stinky and hazy and grim. I cover my face tighter and keep moving up the hill, alongside the road, taking a path as far away from the gas station as possible. When I get to the car, I notice it is parked too close to some shrubs and a wooden fence. I want it as far away from anything flammable as possible. I hop in, start it up, and roll it back a little further, which adds only a few more feet of clearance. Good luck car. Good luck to the few contents we were able to grab. Good luck to what I thought was our way out of here.

I pop open the back, throwing supplies into some reusable grocery bags. I grab a couple more blankets and 3 gallons of water, awkwardly trying to balance it all. I close up the car, beep it locked, and don't look back at it as I head toward the lot and my Andy and our unknown fate, and over a hundred strangers sharing this life changing experience. I watch my steps carefully, juggling the waters and thinking how crazy lucky it was that the distiller broke the day before. I was so frustrated at the time, having to go out and buy plastic bottles, which makes me smile now as I lug them over the dirt path. It really is fascinating how certain things work out; we just don't always have the whole story yet.

As I walk back, I see that It's getting darker and colder, and will be nighttime soon. I try to hustle because being away from Andy even briefly is awful and feels so very wrong in my chest, wrong throughout my entire being. The water jugs are heavy though, digging into my clutching hands, and I move slowly over the dirt path. I would put my current recovery level from the long term illness at about seventy percent. I still have balance and depth perception problems, so I navigate my footing very carefully. Even a lightly sprained ankle can't be allowed to happen out here, not today.

I finally get back to the lot and cross to Building One, unload the jugs of water, and give Andy an extra blanket. He gets up with me, and we go around the building, giving people and their dogs water. Andy assists a woman in a wheelchair that needs him to pick something up for her. We offer dog food to the people near us, but none of the dogs want to eat. They barely drink any water at all and haven't throughout the entire day. It's like they know we shouldn't have to stop and pee; they know we should be running. They know for a certainty that we are in peril. The humans, however, need water to help filter out the smoke. Andy has reminded me to drink water all day long. I refill our canteens after we've handed out what people need. And then we wait again, until I hear my stomach respond to the aftermath of hours of adrenaline. You'd think the body would shut everything down, but that is not always the case. I let Andy know that I have to go to the bathroom and I grab some tissues from my pack. He opts to come with me, to walk the dog, and probably to make sure I'm not out of his sight again.

"The back of Building Two again?" he asks.

"Um, no, that won't work. I need a toilet."

"Good luck with that." We both chuckle.

"No kidding. Let's just get as far away as we can safely, okay?"

We walk across our lot toward a nearby building that is being renovated, The Optimo Lounge. We are far away from the group, but still completely out in the open. It's not like we can go find a tree or bush. They are all gone or still on fire. Live, orange coals are all over the ground on all sides, so we have to remain on the cement slab or surrounding graded construction dirt for safety. I scope out the area, and we keep walking closer to the backside of the Optimo building. Outside of the renovation area are building materials; wood, plywood, some sheet rock, gravel, and miscellaneous random items skewed about. We get closer and I see a tire, a bucket, a new toilet. A freaking toilet, seriously? It's sitting right out in the middle of the gravel lot, proud and mocking. I begin to laugh, a bit of hysteria woven into the cackle.

"Mom." Andy tries to pull me back to sanity, off of the ledge. "Don't." I can't stop laughing. My eyes tear up from it as it continues. He tries again, "Mom."

"No, I am not going to use it Andy. Not like that anyway. But it can provide some privacy. And come on, you have to see the humor in this." I point at the gleaming white porcelain throne balanced on the construction gravel, surrounded by devastation. He looks as if he is trying to see the humor but it escapes him. He shakes his head and turns his back to me, trying to provide additional privacy.

I move over to crouch behind the toilet. *Oh the irony*! My etiquette is stretched perilously thin, but my stomach immediately feels better. Never in a million years did I think this would be my reality, our reality. No one really ever prepares us in advance for just how hard life can be. We just get sidelined with it, with the realities of it.

Andy and I move on, walking a little further, staying on the gravel and away from any trees. We can now partially see our car from where we stand, parked out in the middle of the driveway through the view of the fence. Andy looks to where it was parked before and notices that the side of the Optimo building is on fire, along with some wooden fencing.

"We need to tell someone so they can save that building," he decides.

"Find a firefighter and let them know." Andy is painfully shy and I know it won't be easy for him. He knows I will push him to do it anyway. We walk in silence back to the lot and he finds a firefighter, and briefly shares what he saw. The firefighter nods, thanking Andy for letting him know. Then they leave it, focusing on the gas station and our close surrounding area. Still working with shovels, still keeping people calm.

"Are they just going to let it burn?"

"Maybe, kiddo. They don't seem overly concerned about it right now." It is the closest building to the cement slab on one side. The gas station is on the other side, not on fire but definitely still under threat. We don't yet know the whole situation, don't know exactly why the Optimo isn't being made a priority. We have no idea that the firefighters are keeping information from us to keep the panic and hysteria at bay along with the fire. We don't yet know that they are protecting us from the awful truth they are facing. The truth is that they are fighting with shovels and dirt and axes because they have nothing else. The hydrant closest to us is dry. All of the hydrants are dry. No water is left. No tankers are here. There. Is. No. Water. The Optimo burns.

Chapter 9

And the child grew strong in spirit.

Luke 1:80

We head back to Building One and eat some saltine crackers, nuts, and small bits of beef jerky. Our dinner for tonight. We cuddle, keeping Harley's head covered because otherwise she gets too scared and tries to get away. I remember reading about the animals that all fled the beaches for higher ground before the Sri Lanka tsunami hit shore. They just know somehow, know to get out. Only there is no way out from here. I tuck the blanket around her and she curls up to nap. I ask Andy if he wants to try and rest.

"Not yet," he replies, voice gravelly from smoke and exhaustion. Yeah, me either. Not yet.

Eventually some supplies arrive. First responders check on a woman with a baby. "How much baby food do you have left?" and, "Let us know if you run out". The cherub sits contently in the car seat. The responders announce to all of us that a dispenser of water is being set up with cups in the side area of Building One.

"Try to conserve it folks, that is all we have."

Then they bring in two rolls of toilet paper and put them silently on the ground by the door. People stare at them but no one wants to face this reality. The silence hangs heavy in the air as no one speaks, no one breathes. The toilet paper rolls sit there untouched for a long time, a stark reminder of our current situation. No one wants to be the first to go up there with everyone watching. I send Andy up to grab a wad of it in hopes that it will get other people more comfortable with the idea. He returns with a handful of it and I store it in the backpack in case we need it later. My plan works, and others shuffle up behind him to collect some of the paper. I am tempted to share the location of the random toilet, but I have probably mortified Andy enough for one day.

Andy and I travel around to the people in wheelchairs offering to deliver cups of water when needed. The collective panic has morphed into exhaustion. Faces, hands, and clothing are covered in soot, hair ratted and wild from being covered and uncovered, eyes tired from expressing so much fear, pain, regret.

I tell Andy to sit tight, I have to move around a little, to stretch my body and divert my mind. I promise him I won't leave the cement slab, and he seems to accept that. He holds Harley in his lap, legs crossed, leaning his head back against stacked panels of plywood. I grab my camera, my trusty Cannon, and walk outside. It's my first quality camera, and it has provided a much needed outlet from the realities of parenthood, graduate school, and crisis counseling training. When I look through the lens, everything else temporarily fades away. I love the hunt of the next shot, the change of the lighting, the play of the angles. I walk around the small lot, snapping a few pics, and record a quick video. I watch the firefighters continue the battle armed with shovels and axes. It's like watching a movie. A front row seat to the latest blockbuster. I don't want to be the main character in this flick that is my life right now. But I am. With my kid and dog. *And the Oscar goes to...*

I sigh and let my camera hang off my shoulder. I'm just not able to separate myself and our situation from the photography. All of my other photography has been healing for me, peaceful, and a healthy diversion from our daily stressors. My mind traces back to some of my favorite photos. A worn and faded wooden fence rests on a misty golden pasture, an old rusty red Chevy truck, cool abstracts of bridges everywhere I can manage to visit. Today the viewfinder only brings me closer to the suffering, closer to the fear. I stand and just watch whatever is left continue to smolder. Miraculously, the gas station is still intact. I move forward a few feet more, and am now standing at the edge of the lot, near the road. From behind me I hear the firefighters call everyone over again. I turn back and head over toward Building One. People swarm in quickly, packing in shoulder to shoulder, to try and hear the announcement. I look for Andy, but the crowd is too thick and I can't spot him. I pack up my camera as I walk over and move in against the edge of the crowd to listen.

"Pay attention because I'm only going to say this once," the firefighter yells out to us.
"Bulldozers have cleared Clark road of trees, power lines, and vehicles. We are waiting on a caravan of buses and fire trucks to be organized to come up and get you. Once they can get here, we will load up as many people as possible and begin to get you out of here. We will escort the caravan of buses and trucks for safety. We have no idea when the buses can get here. We will keep you informed as we get updated information."

The crowd immediately begins to murmur, then it breaks apart and people find their way back to their little camps. Thank you God! We all now have a bit of hope. That tiny shimmer powerful enough to keep us going and re-energize our spirits. Everyone still has a thousand questions, but our fire crew only has so much information to share. They are doing an amazing job of keeping everyone calm, of keeping hope alive, of keeping us alive. As people spread out and spaces between the crowds are created, I lock eyes with Andy. He weaves through, making a path toward me.

"Did you get to hear the whole update?"
"I did." He summarizes it again anyway, probably to help him process it all. I listen, processing it myself.

"Yes, exactly, that is my understanding too."

He is considering all of this information, and I recognize the expression he makes when doing mathematical calculations or problem solving. He has questions forming, and I can see those too. I'm pretty sure I am not going to have any answers. He begins the barrage of questioning. Children should be made Grand Inquisitors because they are absolutely relentless. Even at an early age, a child will ask things over and over, unyielding in the quest for answers. Andy poses some really good questions to me, and I am proud that his mind works the way it does. He is trying to figure out options, looking for the best way to face this.

"Andy, all good questions. I wish I had the answers for you, kiddo. I think we just have to wait and see what happens." He doesn't like this, the not knowing. The waiting and not taking action. I don't like it either. I watch him fidget with his fingers and see that he is really struggling with not doing anything to improve our situation.

"Andy, I think you should talk to one of the firefighters about your questions." He looks at me, and I know the concept almost physically pains him. It has always been difficult for him to step out of his comfort zone and I often have to nudge him out of it. He considers it.

"Which one?"

"Pick any of them." I wave my arm out, indicating that he has a selection of firefighters to choose from. He nods, and then shocks me by walking right up to the first firefighter he finds. The firefighter is huge, and Andy is still small for his age. Andy doesn't seem to notice that this guy is not only a hero; he actually looks like a superhero. Or perhaps he does see it. Either way, it doesn't faze him. He stands next to this looming, suited, superhuman and looks up at him. Way up.

"Excuse me," Andy says, his voice still munchkin like. The firefighter leans down to him.

"Yes?"

"So, the condition of Clark road is all clear?"

"Yes, the dozers just finished. There was a lot of debris and some dangerous power lines along with abandoned cars that had to be moved."

"And so now we are just waiting for the buses." Andy phrases this as declarative, not a question.

"Yes, and we will escort them out with our trucks." The firefighter patiently answers, his eyes never leaving Andy's. I remain standing on Andy's right side, not saying anything, just being physically near. This is his conversation to have.

"How long?" Andy asks, and the firefighter knows what he means. We all know what he means. We are all asking the same thing. Will we actually get out of this? Can a caravan of buses really make it up here? How many people can they fit? Who gets to go first? I decide immediately that if children can go on the first load, Andy will be on a bus with or without me. *Please God, just get him out.*

"We don't know. They are trying to get the transportation together now." Still his tone is direct and patient. Still his eyes do not leave Andy's face. Still he leans down. Still he is talking to my son with respect, and compassion, as an equal. Despite the chaos around us, and the thousand other things, critical things, he has to do, he is still all in this conversation with my child. My throat tightens. I will always be grateful to this man for this moment right now.

"So, if the roads are clear right now, and the bulldozers are gone, why are we waiting for the buses when some of us could just drive out now?" Andy's voice is confused, like he is trying to grasp a mathematical calculation or scientific theory that doesn't equate. He truly sounds like the most obvious option is being overlooked, and he can't understand why that is. The firefighter blinks at Andy several times, processing this simplest of scenarios.

"Where is your car, kid?"

Andy points up past the Optimo building, to the left of the street. "It's over there, that is our car right through there. In the lot on the other side." He then points at the street, to the abandoned cars lined up for miles, blocking the road, some of which did not burn. "These are all of our cars," he observes, waving at them and indicating that most of the vehicles within closest proximity actually belong to those of us on this cement slab. The firefighter responds with some type of low sound, a contemplative and curious noise, perhaps even hopeful. Or maybe my kid is inducing a headache, it is difficult to tell.

"Thanks for the idea. For now, just sit tight unless something changes."

"Okay. Thank you."

"You're welcome buddy." He glances at me before turning to walk away. As I smile at this rock star of a human, I'm certain my eyes mist over as I briefly thank him, leaving much unsaid so that he can get back to work saving us all. *Thank you for talking to my son with such respect. Thank you for being a role model for my child, for all of us. Thank you for shoveling dirt onto a freaking wildfire for hours to keep us protected. Thank you for being a patient, compassionate person during a natural disaster. Thank you for being a real life hero.*

I grab Andy and tell him how proud I am that he was able to talk to a stranger and help problem solve. Regardless of what happens, he has something to contribute to the situation and can act on it despite his tendency to want to stay quiet. He is a self-proclaimed introvert, and he is right about it. Yet he was able to move past that today. I hug him tight against me, not letting go, and probably embarrass him with it. Or maybe not. Maybe not today, after all this. He hangs on longer than usual, his head tucked into me. My Andy. We are still standing there a couple of minutes later when they call out the announcement to gather around again. There is a new plan to get us out.

Chapter 10

"I am the light of the world. Whoever follows me will not walk in darkness, but will have the light of life."

John 8:12

We are still standing out on the lot, which perfectly positions us to hear the new announcement. We only have to turn around slightly as the firefighter's voice booms out to call everyone back out for an update. Andy leans against me as we wait for the crowd to form.

"Okay there is a new plan to get everyone out of here. If you can access your vehicle we are going to move you out in groups. Do not leave before your group is called out. We will be grouping based on car location. Some vehicles will have to be moved out of the way first. We are going to do this exactly by the plan. We are going to do this by sections of vehicles. Once you can get to your vehicle, you will drive to the Kmart Parking lot on Clark road. Do not leave Clark Road. Once you get to Kmart you will stay there and wait for instructions. Drive slowly and carefully, there are still hazards to be aware of." People are surprised, and begin to talk amongst themselves as they absorb this new development.

"Does anyone own that white car? It needs to be moved first," one of the firefighters yells from the street. People shuffle around, relaying the message through the crowd. A new energy develops amongst the group; it vibrates and resonates within each of us, and within all of us. It is the smooth sound wave and low hum after a Tibetan bowl chimes. It grows stronger and louder. It is that which manifests within us to accomplish great things, to push us beyond our limits, to go big or go home, to keep fighting. It is the sound of hope.

Or perhaps it isn't a sound at all, this hope and energy we radiate, both singularly and collectively. I change my mind, and decide it is something else entirely. It is not sound. *It is light*. We are all emitting monochromatic light, of a single wavelength and therefore singular color. This is a rarity in physics, but not in miracles. We have been touched by light, by love, and now, hope.

I flash back to years before. The boys and I are driving home from work, school, and preschool. It has been a long day. I am waiting for test results from a biopsy to be processed. My boys are too young to be brought into a discussion about it for now; though that may change depending on the lab results. My trip home with the boys is poignant as the topic of heaven is brought up from their car seats in the back.

"Mommy, what is the color of a soul?" Andy asks out of the blue, stunning me. I remember wondering this myself as a child, though not as young as he is. I maneuver the mountain roads as the questions threaten to stall my brain like an old car with a flooded engine. How do I answer this? It's a simple yet astronomically huge question. How much is he able to comprehend? Is he randomly curious or does this need to be a whole conversation? Questions can travel through a mother's mind faster than the speed of light. It's a well-known but undocumented occurrence that Stephen Hawking overlooks in all of his theories. The speed of maternal processing of hypothetical questions.

"What color do you think they are?" I ask, truly interested.

"Maybe blue like the angels," Andy answers.

"Angels aren't blue," Tommy chimes in. A heated debate ensues, my three and six year olds both adamant. Andy describes angels as, "glowing a bluish light, wearing flowing long material, with wings that are not of any feathers we have seen. Feathery, but not like bird feathers. And they are the most beautiful thing you have ever seen."

Tommy then describes angels as, "having golden hair, but with light in and around it. The hair is curls, more curls than Nanny," which is his pronunciation and subsequent nickname for Andy. "And the curls are so long, hanging down. Angels have golden light all around. Yellowish gold."

"No, it is blue, I have seen it," Andy demands.

"So have I and it is gold," Tommy insists.

They are both adamant. I am in awe of this whole conversation. How do they think this, know this at such an early age? How could they believe so fiercely about how angels look? And then it dawns on me. They are telling the absolute truth, their truth, as they are both too young to know anything but what the truth is. They speak only brutal honesty at this age and everything is matter of fact. Something about their innocence, their youth and inexperience, allows them to know in a way that is effortless, as part of their being. Adults strive for years to gain faith on this level.

"What if you are both right?" This gets their attention immediately and silences the debate. I see their wide eyes in the rearview mirror, this concept incomprehensible.

"Huh?" Andy asks, incredulous.

"Maybe you saw different angels. Maybe Angels are all different colors. Maybe there are colors in the universe that we don't even know about yet." I see their faces as this sinks in and they consider it. *Mind blown.*

And that is how I feel right now on this charred cement slab, mind blown, in this moment of light and hope and love. The light energy swirls around us, through us, from us, like a Patronus, glowing and protective. Two hundred souls shining radiant, as one. E pluribus unum. Out of many, one. We are one.

And then the light moves, scatters about, and we have to separate. The moment passes and everyone begins to move around. Andy and I hustle. I wave at him, probably somewhat frantically, to head back into Building One. It may look like I am wild eyed and flailing my arms, but he comprehends what I am signaling. My boys are amazing at deciphering my expressions, sounds, gestures. He knows exactly what I am communicating to him. He is probably thinking it at the same time. *Go. Now. While we still have the chance. Move before they change their minds.*

"Let's go, grab our stuff," I yell to him over the noises of the crowd, still stunned at the sudden change of events. New adrenaline pumps through me and I am no longer exhausted. We pack up our small camp, our bodies loaded with our backpacks, blankets, bags.

We move back out to the slab and wait for our group to be called.

"Stay close, Andy," I warn. It is still far from safe as we watch the firefighters direct people to their cars a few at a time. Slowly, so painfully slowly, vehicles are being moved. Time has decelerated again, and we watch as the process takes far too long. But still, it is something. A tiny glimmer of hope to cling to, gradually growing brighter. I look over at the gas station. The wooden fence adjacent to it is burning. Driving right past it is the only way out.

Eventually our group of vehicles gets the clearance to go ahead and leave the slab. We hike up the dirt path along the road, still unable to comprehend the mass destruction all around us. We point out random and horrific things as we travel up the path; a barber shop sign on fire, remnants of cars, trees still burning, downed power lines, smoldering piles that used to be homes. The scenery looks like those photographs that are black and white except for a bit of color left in for dramatic flair. A black and white rainy day and a red umbrella. A grayscale woman with red lips. Only this landscape is black trees, white ash, gray charcoal, and orange flames and coals.

We reach the car safely and I quickly look it over, circling it from front to back. Bumpers and lights are still intact at both ends. The side mirrors are fine. Ash and debris are all over it, but the tires look fine and nothing seems to have melted off at a glance. At this point anything mobile would pass my inspection standards. It will have to be good enough to get us out of here. We unload all of our packs and blankets, shoving it all into the back, not wasting any time. I load up Harley, and tell Andy to hook her harness to the latch tether. "Let's roll," I say, looking at him. He nods, and we drive toward the road, maneuvering around cars, debris, power lines, and fire. We slowly head directly toward the gas station.

Chapter 11

God can turn around any situation.

Romans 8:28

The car crawls over and through debris and abandoned cars until we get down near the intersection at Clark and Skyway. The cement slab is on our right; the gas station is on the left. We barely creep forward, and it doesn't escape me that we are in the worst spot possible if the station blows. I watch the burning fence near the gas station most of the way as we slowly drive around the corner. My guess is they are letting us go because if it blows the risk is just too high. We finally get past the station, but no sigh of relief comes. We drive over power lines across the road, and under power lines that are sagging low with power poles that have burned from the ground up, the top parts of the poles still on fire and hanging from the wires. I snap a pic of one that looks like a cross, burning and weighing down the lines. Trees lining the road are barely standing, the trunks burning almost completely through. I stop and wait to move forward until we have enough clearance to pass the most hazardous ones, praying that they do not fall and hit us or block the road. As we get further down the road, I realize that all of these people should probably not be driving in this, it is still much too dangerous. We all keep going anyway.

I have never seen a war zone first hand, but I'm pretty certain this level of ruin can normally only be accomplished by a bomb detonation. Skeletons of cars are frozen in ash. Trees that should be giants are blackened twigs, some burning down through the stump and roots, leaving holes in the ground like little land mines. With so many trees gone, the now desolate landscape is visible for miles, and it looks like a vast cemetery of chimneys. The brick fireplaces stand lonely and forsaken, the only things that remain upright in the ashes. It is dark now, and I can't tell where we are. Nothing is familiar on this road that I have traveled so many times, days, years. No landmarks remain.

    My heart is breaking but I can't cry yet, I still have to drive us out of this. I focus on the road, the debris, the intense heat from the fire that we feel through the glass of the windows and windshield. I try to only look straight ahead but I can't ignore what is all around us. It is absolute devastation, ground zero, nothingness. Worse than nothingness because of what it used to be. Paradise, as far as the eye can see, obliterated. *It is just all gone.*

    We are finally able to recognize that we are getting into town. The movie theatre is unscathed, the huge cement lot serving as a protective barrier. We keep driving, close to the Kmart parking lot now. Many of the cars pull into the lot. I follow the parade with my blinker on. As we get closer to the turn, I see a white fire truck heading straight and staying on Clark Road. There is another fire truck parked in the street just past the Kmart entrance to the lot. As soon as I see the firefighter standing outside of the truck, my decision is made and I pass the parking lot turn and slowly drive up toward him.

    "Mom…" Andy is about to tell me I missed the turn. But I have to try this. I just have to ask.

    "Andy, I know, hang on a sec, I just have to ask him for a status update."

    "Okay," he replies as I slow to a stop in the middle of the dark, deserted street.

    I roll down my window and the firefighter walks right over.

"I know we are supposed to go in to the Kmart lot, but I just saw the truck up ahead and thought I'd ask for an update," I tell him.

"Where are you heading?" he asks, nodding.

"Chico."

"You have a place to stay with someone?"

"Yes, we are going to see my other son and his father." I indicate Andy in the backseat with my head. The firefighter looks over at him. Perhaps he sees our desperation. Perhaps he is a father himself. I will never know what exactly prompts him to respond how he does.

"You can go through, but stay on Clark Road only. Do not for any reason turn off of Clark. Skyway is not safe. Stay on Clark." He is adamant, and I nod profusely. I will agree to most anything right now, just get us off this mountain. Get us back to my Tommy. "I promise. We will stay on Clark."

"Okay, follow that truck. Be safe."

"Thank you so much!" I tell him, and Andy says thanks before I roll up the window and pull away, looking back at all the cars still parked at Kmart, at the long line of cars still turning into that lot. We follow the white truck for a while but then it fades in the distance, the darkness swallowing the taillights whole. A car is behind us and I think maybe they are letting people through, either that or this driver somehow survived and is now going to try to get out. We come to the intersection of Elliot Road, drive through it, and see the car turning right and heading toward Skyway.

"Why would they go that way?" Andy asks me, concerned.

"I don't know kiddo," I reply. "Not a good idea."

"Will they be okay?"

"I hope so." I just don't have all the answers today. The car's headlights disappear and we are alone on the road again, with no other vehicles in sight for miles. I have a brief moment of trepidation over this, but shake it off quickly. This is not the time to panic. This is our path right now. I keep driving.

As we drive, we see our hangouts, the businesses we frequent, our favorite places to eat. They are on fire.

"Oh no," I say, as we approach Pearson Road.

"Oh man, the Foster's Freeze," Andy says in response. "At least Tommy doesn't have to see that."

"Yeah," I agree. But we have to see it. That was our special hangout place with my Gramps before he passed. My kids, their great grandfather, great grandmother, grilled burgers, and ice cream cones dipped in chocolate. The memories can't burn up but my heart breaks a little more seeing it on fire, knowing it is gone now too. This fire has changed everything. Thick tears blur my vision. I blink rapidly. I am tempted to lose it right now and just let the powerful emotions of the day escape my body. But I still have to keep it together. I still have to try to get us out of this.

We pass a cell tower, and it prompts me to frantically dig out my phone. Maybe, just maybe. I place a call to the boys' father, Ken. The line is silent, and my phone screen shows the word "dialing" for way too long. I wait anyway, willing it to connect. It takes over a full minute to even begin to dial.

Ken and I have had a rough go of it and don't get along very well. But that doesn't keep me from empathizing his experience in this. I can't imagine being on the other end of this situation. Wondering for hours upon hours if your child is alive with no new information to go on. To get a call from your ex's colleague saying the last message received is that we have to proceed on foot. From a monstrous wildfire. And then hear nothing for over six hours. To watch the news show horrific footage and begin to compile even more horrific statistics. To hear from neighbors who left after we did but were able to get down to Chico before us. To have everyone call and ask how we are and have no good response to share. To just sit and wait and know that your other child is waiting too. To watch your youngest cry and ask questions and refuse to sleep.

I think of my mom, who was also evacuating today, though the threat was likely less in her area if the winds brought the beast our way instead. She must be frantic with no news from us. Her daughter and grandson. She knows I would get word out if I could. Everyone knows that I would communicate our status if we had any way to get a message out. They all know it's unlikely that we are alive at this point, and yet they all wait, calling every twenty minutes around the clock to check for news on our whereabouts. My mom calls the police, the fire department, the hospital, and even the local news trying to get information. No one has anything to share.

The broken dialing tone of my cell brings me back to the call, and I hear my ex answer frantically, his voice sounding as if he is not sure I am actually calling. I tell him quickly that we are driving now, that we will likely lose the call. He responds, but is in shock still from the whole situation. I can hear it in his voice. He shares that we have to drive to Oroville, that Highway 99 is closed. Many people are staying in Oroville for the night. I tell him I will find a way around, that whatever it takes we will get to Chico, to see him and Tommy, tonight. I almost lose it at the thought of seeing Tommy, of the boys being together, of us making it out of this alive. I choke back a sob and take a slow breath. *Just drive.*

"Call my mom," I begin to tell him, but I am interrupted by a long, low beep. The call is dropped. I hand it back to Andy so he can try to keep reaching people, but we don't manage to get any other calls out. Knowing that Ken will be passing on the information via phone tree to my family, I turn my concentration back to the dark and dangerous path before us. We aren't out of here yet.

The road gets really rough right outside of town. Power lines are down all over the road, looking like long deadly snakes; thick debris is scattered everywhere. *Thump, thump.* We drive over a large charred branch, jostling the vehicle. Sparks flit up into the air all around the car, little orange streaks stark against the blackest night. No streetlights, no headlights, no businesses, no homes. Just sparks in the darkness. *Thump.* I grip the steering wheel so tightly I am probably going to leave marks in the leather from my rings. I pray again and keep driving.

We pass the Paradise airport and get a clear view of the hills for miles, on the way down to Butte College. I gasp and gesture to my phone.

"Andy, see if you can capture that," I tell him over my shoulder. He aims it out the window and takes some pics. The hills look like they are covered in lava. Flowing, seeping lava is all we can see for miles and miles and miles. Hill after hill on fire, overlapping other hills, covered in glowing red blobs everywhere. It is the only light being emitted. No moonlight, no stars. The smoke blocks it all out. The enormity of the mass destruction hits me and my stomach drops. Andy is silent as we just take it all in, dumbfounded. My heart can't break any further right now so it just goes numb.

We eventually get past Butte College and approach Durham Dayton Road, the first route to Chico, and it is closed. To the far right of us, police personnel and multiple barricades are on site. Since we can't go that way, I continue straight ahead instead, cruising slowly through the intersection. I'm hoping we won't get stopped or pulled over and questioned, but no one seems to notice our one lone car making the treacherous drive out, unescorted.

We stay on 191, which is the bottom end of Clark road, and head toward Oroville. At least now we are out of the flames. The smoke is still thick and the car stinks terribly but we can't roll down the windows, it is much worse outside. We merge onto Highway 70, and we immediately see closure signs for Highway 149, which is the route over to Highway 99 and the way back to Chico. I check the gas level. I think we can get to Oroville.

Gas stations are probably not too impacted in Oroville. My plan is to get there, gas up, and then find a path, any path, back to Chico. The north end of Chico wouldn't be blocked off. Even if I have to circle way around and take back roads an hour or two or three out of the way, I will see Tommy tonight. There has to be a way.

We continue driving on Highway 70, and see the green highway signs for 149. I slow and see that the closure sign is there, but it doesn't completely block the road. There are no police personnel on site, it all looks deserted. Is the road open? There is no one to ask. I stop the car, right there in the middle of the highway. I look around, assessing the situation. There is no fire around us now, no immediate threat that I can identify or imagine. If we get to 99 and they have it barricaded I guess we just turn around. It's worth a shot, and it just feels like the right way to go. I slowly turn right and maneuver onto 149, still the only car, the only headlights, for miles. We travel on the deserted highway, toward 99, toward safety, toward my Tommy. We finally make it to Highway 99.

On a typical night, Highway 99 is always full of traffic. Even in the middle of the night, cars and semi-trucks travel this route as a main thoroughfare It leads to the Sacramento Airport, and a myriad of other places, making it full of traffic around the clock. But this is not a typical night. I survey the lanes, looking through the smoke for what might be miles, it is difficult to judge. There are still no other cars heading in either direction. Is this road still closed and we just don't know it? Where is all of the traffic? Where are all of the other evacuees? This looks like an old desert highway that no one ever uses anymore. Or what you might see in Hollywood after the Zombie Apocalypse. This highway is normally bumper to bumper at 5:00 p.m. The view is so bizarre, as if this whole thing might just be a horrible nightmare and any moment I will wake from it, sitting up in bed sweaty and shaking and so grateful it was just a dream. I don't wake up, so I keep driving.

From the highway we can see the massive orange glow of the fire ceilinged by the black smoke. The light of the fire is trapped under the canopy of what looks like an atomic bomb cloud. It is unfathomable, consuming the entire landscape, for miles and miles and miles. It is still burning, still moving. I hit the accelerator and we fly on the highway, no cars to slow us down, no traffic to have to pass.

"Um, Mom, how fast are we going?" Andy tries to lean forward from the backseat but luckily can't see the speedometer from his vantage point.

"Pretty fast baby," I respond honestly, checking my speed. It's the fastest I've ever driven this car, the fastest I've driven any car. Pretty damn fast. Go Toyota.

"But what if we get a ticket?" He knows I have never been ticketed for speeding. He knows that I don't break the law, that I respect our law enforcement and the laws in general. We have also never almost died in a wildfire, driven through Hell, and been separated from Tommy during a treacherous, near death experience. He is also figuring out that the speed limit doesn't apply to us right now. They can follow me and ticket us when we get there. I am not slowing down and I am not stopping. Not tonight.

"We won't get a ticket Andy. There are no cops out here right now. There is no one out here right now, look around. There is nothing." He glances out the window and all we see are the occasional overhead highway lights through the smoky darkness. I can almost pretend it's just thick fog. Almost.

I don't let off the gas, not even a little. We have enough fuel to get us there, even burning through it like this. We cruise alone at high altitude just above the fast lane. My head throbs, my eyes ache, my lungs and throat burn. A migraine is in my near future. I see the sign for the Chico city limit. Almost, Tommy. Hang on, baby boy. We are almost there.

"Andy, that's the sign for Chico," I point, probably to convince myself more than to convince him. T-minus fifteen minutes. Maybe less." Probably less at this speed.

"Okay," he replies, his voice scratchy and tired.

"We need to pray our thanks, kiddo. We prayed to ask for help, and now we need to send a thank you prayer," I tell him.

"I already did, Mom," he says.

"Okay, that's good." My heart swells. I have taught him this, I have done this part right. He will have this forever, with or without me. I hope I recover fully from this illness, because I have so much more to do, but knowing that he can pray on his own and understands what it is all about is a blessing of peace in my heart. *Thank you, God. Thank you, God. Thank you, God.*

We begin to pass the green freeway Chico exit signs. Exit 383, Park Avenue/Skyway/Paradise. *Paradise.* I wonder when I will take that route next. It's going to be longer than I think. Don't think about that yet. Just drive. Exit 384, 20th Street. Just keep going. Exit 385, Highway 32. One more. Exit 386, Chico State/East 1st Avenue. I pull into the exit lane and onto the off ramp. *We got this.*

We drive through town, retracing a path I've driven thousands of times. A path I've driven for years. I was born in this town, these are my old streets, my old hangouts. But this time is different than all the others. This time is a gift, an immeasurable blessing. We came so close to not being here, to not traveling this path. We almost didn't make it out. Almost roasted in a Pepsi trailer. Almost burned in our car, or trying to escape the fire on foot. Almost suffocated from the smoke. It was almost the last time we saw everyone we loved. But God has other plans. We will get to see loved ones again. Tommy comes first.

Chapter 12

Then you will call on me and come and pray to me, and I will listen to you.

Jeremiah 29:12

We finally arrive at Ken's house and none of it seems possible. It's been a day of forevers. Drive forever, huddle on that cement slab forever, and then drive forever again. We walk in, and Tommy runs to me, clutching on to me, allowing my heart to stop breaking. I want this forever.

"Mommy, I remembered!"

"Remembered what, baby?" I can't imagine what he could have forgotten that is so important that it's the first thing he tells me about after this kind of ordeal.

"I remembered to pray!" he exclaims. Oh, my heart. How can my heart take this? It's been so through much today it seems impossible that I can feel anything. But I do. I feel my heart swell with happiness at his happiness, pride at his pride, love for his love. I feel exactly what is in his heart, mirrored in mine and magnified exponentially. This is how a mother's love feels. It feels what our children feel. Grieves at their losses and celebrates at their joys. Their hearts are in our hearts.

I think back to months ago. Six months, maybe more. I am in bed for the evening, exhausted from the illness at an early hour. The boys are in bed. It is peaceful up on the hill.

"Mommy," I hear a soft munchkin voice. Tommy crawls up onto my huge bed.

"Mommy, I'm so sad," he whispers.

"Why sweetheart?" I ask, concerned about what is bothering him at night. "Did you have a bad dream? I wrap him in my arms and he lays against me, warm and small and soft.

"No, sometimes I just feel like I am a bad kid," he shares. He is crying.

"Tommy, no, you are an amazing kid. Why would you ever think that? Please tell me about this."

"Sometimes when I am away from you I forget to pray." His voice is muffled and his little body clings to me, his head tucked down into my side.

"Tommy, listen to Mommy. Look at me. You are only eight years old, you are still learning. And it's a habit to pray here with me, because we do it every day, so it helps us remember. When you are away from that, away from me, it isn't as easy to remember. It does not make you a bad kid at all. God understands all of this. When you get older, you will remember it more. And I bet if there was something really important, you would remember to pray."

"Promise?" His tear filled eyes are big and beautiful.

"Promise." He snuggles into me, his little arms around me, holding me tight. I stroke his fine, silky hair and feel his warm body relax into mine as he falls asleep. He still has that sweet baby smell, like sugar cookies or a cupcake. I love this child so much.

His current excitement pulls me back into the present. He is looking up at me, clinging to me, the most loving person I have ever known.

"I remembered to pray! I was so scared, and you didn't call and you didn't call some more and then I finally remembered to pray and two minutes later you called and now you are here." That's all it takes for me to completely lose it. I have no words, only sobs as the horror of the day has to escape my body somehow. I am overwhelmed with the gratitude that fills me. I get to keep hugging my kids, get to keep being Mommy. It is my most favorite thing ever. We get more time, more us. It is the greatest gift from above that I could ever imagine.

"Mommy, is that happy tears?" he asks to make sure.

"It is, baby. I am crazy happy to see you. And I knew you would remember to pray. I just knew it." I can't let go of him. Andy comes over to us after hugging Ken and we all just stand there, hugging each other, not saying anything. I can't believe we survived that, made it out. None of it makes sense to me. The entire day was wrong. Or was it? This part, this moment, is the most right thing I have ever felt.

Ken walks over to us. I begin to tell him that it was so, so awful, but I choke back sobs instead of getting all the words out. "You guys are here now," he says, exhaling a deep breath. "And you guys stink." I can't smell it, our noses probably incapable of detecting anything after being exposed to the smoke for so long. I look at Andy, and realize his face is covered in black soot. In fact, he is covered everywhere in soot except for the area the little hood protected around his nose, mouth, and chin. Our hands are blackened and I can feel the fine grit all over my skin.

"Andy can shower first," I say, looking over at him. He looks too exhausted to argue it.

"Wash everything three times, kiddo."

He nods and drags himself down the hallway, shuffling into the bathroom, and out of my sight for the second time today. I hate it. I want him pressed to me, right next to me. He is too far away. I sit and wait, and Tommy climbs up onto my lap. We sit like that, and I listen to the sounds of the shower to check on Andy. Shower curtain. The squeak of the shower knobs being twisted. Water hitting the tub drain. The squeak of the pull, then water falling. Shower curtain again. Water. *Shhhhhhhhhhhh.* Shampoo bottle lid. *Click, squirt, snap.*

He finally comes out, three shades less sooty. He is pale and looks awful. I hug him. "You okay?" I ask. He nods once, probably too tired to even respond. I head toward the bathroom and peel off my smoke infused clothes. I catch a glimpse of my reflection and *oy vey*. My hair looks like I have been electrocuted. It stands out wildly in all directions, with gnarly tangles and lumps. It must have been from the fleece blanket, on and off, covering our heads, and then the heat trapped under it. *Wowzer*. My entire face and neck are blackened from soot, eyes glassy and disbelieving; the look of shock apparent in my expression. What the hell happened today? Is this real? I find a brush, dragging it through the knots as best I can, and step into the shower, scrubbing as hard and as quickly as I can. I don't want to be away from the boys for one minute longer than is absolutely necessary.

    I get out, towel off, and blow my nose. Black particles speckle the mucous all over the tissue, looking like death confetti. This is a party I don't want to attend. We were breathing all of that in for over six hours. I notice that my face is really red, like a bad sunburn. It is tender and even touching my lips is painful. Maybe from the heat, or maybe from the wind. Maybe from both.

    I gather up our clothes and the dog blankets to throw in the wash. The smell is atrocious. Deep, pungent smoke. But not like a campfire, not like cigarettes. This is rotten, putrid smoke and it is so powerful. I contemplate just throwing everything away, but it's all we have until we can get back home. My socks have a pattern from being soot ridden, white rings present everywhere there was a crease or scrunch. I dump everything into the machine, shoes too. It takes three scalding hot washes with extra rinses for the smell to be removed.

    I find Ken and ask for a sweatshirt to borrow. It's that or keep wearing this t-shirt with no bra. He finds one, and hands it over, standing as far away as he can within reaching distance. I thank him, pull it over my head, and then we just stare at each other for a moment. *Awkward*. He looks like he is thinking he will need to get rid of the sweatshirt later. I am not happy about this either. I'm in my ex's hoodie, braless.

Gak. But we are both too relieved to say anything, too relieved to care.

9:15 p.m.

It is late, but we haven't eaten much all day. We basically never felt hungry, but instead forced down crackers and some jerky just knowing that we had to. We all sit elbow to elbow at the small, round kitchen table. My ex mother-in-law has made an amazing chicken soup. She comes from a long line of Sicilian chefs and restaurateurs. Normally the soup would have no chance. Tonight, however, Andy and I only sip at it slowly. We should be ravenous, but we both feel sick. Our lungs and throats are burning. We have headaches and nausea. Achy muscles. Exhaustion. No one speaks, because words don't suffice at a time like this. Andy and I can't discuss what it was like for us, and the others can't express what it was like on their side either. No words are powerful enough to represent the emotions of nearly dying and then being reunited with loved ones. They do not exist in any language. As we continue to try and eat, the only sounds are the faint clinking of the spoons against the bowls, and the background noise of the television, the news covering the mass destruction of the fire's wake.

We manage to eat some soup and bread, and we drink more water. The pain in my head worsens, like someone is hitting it over and over with a hard object. All of us want this day to be over, for the nightmare of it to end and not be our reality anymore. Everyone clears the dishes and says their goodnights. The boys and I head to the back room they share here and crawl into the bottom bunk, the three of us somehow managing to balance on the small mattress with the dog. I already know I will be awake tonight. Sleep is not going to be an option.

I'm still too hyperactive internally from the adrenaline of the drive. I say our prayers, the boys just listening tonight. Usually we all contribute, adding our pleases and thank yous and love yous. Tonight is different; they are already half asleep on me. My head throbs but we are reunited. We survived. We are all alive and together and holding each other. I lie as still as I can, trying not to disrupt this moment of peace that surrounds us. I manage this for a couple of hours, just breathing them in and listening to their breathing and giving thanks.

Then a buzzing alarm sounds on my cell phone. It's not the alarm clock, not a call, not a message. It is the emergency notification system. This area, our current location, is now under voluntary evacuation. The fire has burned all the way down the hill, completely through Paradise, through the canyon, and is approaching Chico city limits. *No. It cannot be.*

Chapter 13

Under His wings, you will find refuge.

Psalm 91:4

My mind replays the emergency notification for evacuation. It is voluntary, not mandatory, but that could rapidly change. So now what do we do? Re-evacuate? To where? Maybe we should just make the five hour drive over to the coast and wait it all out by the ocean. That would probably help our lungs, help our souls, to heal from today. All of those negative ions entering the body, brain, and bloodstream. Flowing through our cells, lowering blood pressure and increasing immunity. I need a jar of ocean air right now, cleansing and pure. To clear my body, clear my mind. I need to think this situation through.

    Chico has a city fire department that is dedicated to the protection of the town. They don't leave to fight other fires. They stay here, 24/7/365, to protect everything within the city lines. *No matter what.* I envision the area that is under threat right now. There are no more forested pines, just occasional oak trees. It is a grassy, rocky terrain for quite some distance before homes begin to speckle the landscape. It will be a grass fire, which burns quickly, but nothing like a forest fire in terms of gaining momentum or rate of destruction. The golf course homes are being evacuated now because of the close proximity to the burning areas. We are probably one whole zone away from that. Maybe two.

    Evacuating Chico would not be like evacuating Paradise. There are so many ways out, and only a few areas that could even burn once the residential areas are reached.

And it's not like we need to pack anything. We can just get in the car and go if the call comes through. I decide that we will wait for an update, to let the boys sleep a little. The television is still on in the living room, and I assume that my ex is probably not getting much rest either. I lie there in bed and wait, praying.

Faith is an interesting thing. As physical beings, we are used to the tangible, used to limitations. Everything is measured. Time, weight, mass, distance. We strive to explain it all. The invisible, inexplicable, the immeasurable, are all counterintuitive to everything we see here on Earth. So how is it that humans can have faith, something opposite our immediate surroundings here? For me, there are moments, blessings, that are sensed, that are felt. *I just know.*

I close my eyes, not to sleep, but to rest my mind, to just know, to just be. I hear something faint, something being carried in on the wind. Honks, out of rhythm. Many low, soft honks. This is a sound from my childhood out in the country, a sound of the world still spinning, life still living. It is the sound of the snow geese flying overhead. Is it migration time already? Are they fleeing? The timing seems wrong to me, it is too early in the season, too warm for this to happen yet.

Their calls are both haunting and peaceful. Not a song, but a message. They speak to each other, and they speak to my weary soul. I strain to hear every last bit of the fading honks. It fills my heart and I know there is so much more to this life and beyond. *I just know.* I know tonight that it is all going to be okay. I know tonight that the boys and I are together, and I feel the love and protection that has surrounded us all day long. I know tonight that we get to have tomorrow, all of us together.

I continue to lie there, wanting to focus on gratitude and prayer, but my body is overcome with a feeling of sickness. My head is still pounding and my heart races from nausea. I need to head into the bathroom, but I am worried that moving will wake the boys. They need to sleep. At first I think it is the headache causing the stomach upset. I soon realize that is not the case. I feel like I have been poisoned. And in a way, I have been. By the smoke. With smoke poisoning, fine particulates are inhaled through the respiratory system and enter the bloodstream. And this wasn't just smoke. It was paint, asbestos, cleaning products, plastics, vehicles, and a myriad of other toxins that were incinerated and blown into the air all around us. I drag myself out from under the boys and dog, down the hall and into the bathroom. The vomiting begins with a vengeance and lasts through the remainder of the night.

Once the vomiting subsides, I return to bed again. Both of the boys have nightmares. The puppy has nightmares. She whimpers and twitches, probably trying to make a run for it even in sleep. Andy sits straight up in the bed and tells me we need to evacuate. He is still asleep, eyes glazed over, and will not remember it tomorrow. Tommy clings to me every time I shift, saying, "Don't go Mommy." I am physically, mentally, and emotionally spent. My muscles, my mind, and my heart all ache a little. I lie awake until the sunlight just barely graces the window. Only then, in the smoky, early dawn, do I allow myself to drift to sleep. It is fitful, filled with nightmares of my own.

Later in the morning, the previous night's vomiting is followed immediately by bowel problems and no appetite. I am sick. Andy is sick. The dog is sick. We cannot eat. I try to sip some coffee and have to leave it. Andy sits at the table for breakfast, also unable to eat. He is silent today, and has said nothing out loud since we arrived here last night.

Despite being ill, I make arrangements for my family to come and see us. They arrive in packs, hugging and kissing us and crying and not letting go. I hear the stories of their evacuations, find out where everyone is staying, because all of the homes spanning our three towns are still under threat. We have no family to stay with, because the whole family has been evacuated. Old friends are called, spare rooms are set up, prayers are made. We all just wait to hear about when the fire might be contained. As of right now, it doesn't look good. We learn from the news that that it spread at an incomprehensible speed, and shows no sign of stopping.

    The next few days are the same. We try to eat, drink water, try to sleep. Our faces begin peeling, mine a little worse than Andy's, though his eyebrow area is pretty bad. Both of us have cracked and peeling lips that bleed. It takes Andy three full days before he begins to speak out loud, four days before he can begin to eat small meals, and another day or two before he laughs. When I hear it escape his mouth, it is a beautiful sound, with high, lilting peals not yet impacted by puberty. It resonates, sweet and healing, within me. He is laughing, speaking, eating. *Thank you God.*

    House arrest for the city and beyond continues. We play bingo, play with the puppy, and play board games to help try and pass the time. There is no escaping the current reality of our situation, though. With the rest of the world, we watch the news, watch the perimeter of the fire spread and spread, like spilled liquid, edging out in all directions. A living, evil Rorschach that isn't fully formed yet. Containment is not an option under the current conditions. It is hot, dry, and windy. The years of drought status are now the perfect fuel for a wildfire and there is just no stopping it. We watch the death toll rise. We watch the missing persons list grow. We hear about structures incinerated, businesses gone, homes destroyed, lives lost. The boundary of the fire eats its way up the mountain side, the maps online and on television giving us a general idea of what is gone.

    Paradise has been decimated. Parts of Jarbo Gap and Concow and other surrounding areas have also been damaged. The fire continues to push through everything. It is moving through lower Magalia, toward my grandmother's house. Toward our street. Toward our neighbors' property. Toward our little house on the hill. Toward our home. We wait.

Chapter 14

Do not be afraid; do not be discouraged, for the Lord your God will be with you wherever you go.

Joshua 1:9

The waiting to hear about our house is excruciatingly heavy on our shoulders, on our minds, on our souls. We all feel the weight of it bearing down on us like increased gravity. The entire city of Chico is on lockdown because of the density of the smoke. It is dark and cold all day long because the sun can't get through. Schools all around us are closed. This means parents everywhere are either staying home from work or are making accommodations. Parks are empty. Sidewalks deserted. Because the colleges are also closed, my work is on hold. We all just hang around and wait. Wait for the containment to begin. Wait for the word about our home. Wait to make a plan.

While we wait, we all need extra clothing and personal care items, so my family meets and visits one of the shelters set up at the local Elks Lodge. It is a cold, smoky evening. The volunteers take our information and immediately provide safety masks for breathing. I strap one on to my face and adjust the metal nose crimp and then try to place my glasses over the mask. They steam up every time I exhale. Through the foggy lenses, I survey the area. Table after table, row after row, is set up with looming piles of clothes. The donation site is enormous. I wander through in a daze, finding an essential item here and there. Clothes for the boys first: sporty shorts, tshirts, pants. A set of Under Armour hoodies, brand new. A few things for me when they appear in the piles: a hoodie from a surf shop in Hawaii, soft and blue. A fleece scarf, gray. A pair of yoga pants, black. A faded pair of low rise jeans with the knee blown out and designed for someone twenty years younger. No socks. No underwear. All of the local stores are out of these as well. No women's panties for miles and miles.

    I dig through a box of travel sized toiletries: shampoo, soap, deodorant, razor. A volunteer approaches me, kind and gentle. She holds out a blue ski jacket to me and says, "you are shivering and this looks like it might be your size." I thank her and put it on, noticing it is dark now and we are digging through clothing by spotlights. Most of the other evacuees have already left or are heading for the parking lot. I'm ready to leave too and to feel less grief, to see less suffering, to experience a better reality than this. If we get some rest tonight, if we can recharge our spirits just a bit, we can come back and face this again tomorrow.

    With no word yet on the house, and no access for anyone to return to Paradise, we have to remain in Chico. There are no hotels, so my family and I decide to stay with a good friend of my mother's. The term friend really doesn't do her justice. This woman is a superhero, a dynamo, a word of awesomeness that hasn't even been invented yet. She takes in all of us for days that turn into weeks. My mom, brother, grandmother, cousin, auntie, and the boys and I. And Harley, and my brother's dog. She feeds us home cooked meals, prepares snacks, drives us to and from the shelters to collect clothing, helps us find said clothing, washes it all and labels it for us in piles, makes us laugh, and hugs us when we cry. Her hubby spends his days volunteering at the shelters with the Red Cross. No thank you will ever suffice.

    The days all blur into one long day, and I don't even know what day of evacuation we are on, I have lost track at this point. While we are not having to camp out in a tent like some, or cars like others, we still look and feel like refugees.

The thing is, even staying at people's homes, it is still not our own space. It is not my bed, my pillows, my shower, my stuff. Everyone's house makes different sounds, has different smells, has a different feel. I soon realize that every refrigerator has a unique sound, every heating system its own hum, the walls their own creaks, and the foreign noises distract me from sleep, from peace.

I head out to my car to gather up a few essentials; shampoo, soap, socks. My car is filthy and still smells of smoke inside. Whatever. I can't expend the energy it would take to care about that right now. I rifle through and find the plastic bag from the local CVS pharmacy with my favorite coconut shampoo and sensitive skin wash. I am looking forward to using something familiar, using something of mine, something that smells like home.

I load up my bags and close up the car, not wanting to linger too long in the smoky air. My mom is standing next to her car, which is parked in front of mine on the street, talking on the phone. She hangs up just as I shut my car door and am heading toward the house. She has received bad news, I can tell immediately. It is all over her face, that face that I can read at any given time. I walk up to her.

"Hey," I say to her, my arms full of the donated stuff from the shelters and my soon to be shower kit.

"I have some bad news," she says, wincing. Well, this isn't good. She looks stricken, and adrenaline pumps through me. Did someone pass away? The toll is so high I'm sure we will know someone who didn't make it out. I don't want to hear it.

"That was your neighbors, Gene and Kelly, on the phone. You lost the house. I'm so sorry. I wish it could have been my house instead." She wraps her arms around me, and I stand there, frozen and stunned. We lost the house. It repeats slowly in my mind, over and over, but not sinking in all the way. We lost the house.

"It's okay," I tell her, straightening my back to shift the weight of the world into a more balanced position on my shoulders. "Andy and I made it out alive. That's all that matters." I know it is the truth, and my mom knows it too. She doesn't respond as tears fill her eyes. I need a moment to hyperventilate, so I turn away and head into the house, somewhat dazed. I enter the doorway and use every bit of strength I have to keep a poker face when I meet my grandmother's eyes. She is sitting on the couch, hands in lap, clutching a tissue, weeping over the television broadcasting only sad news. She doesn't need to know this yet. We are still waiting to hear about her place. The loss of our home was confirmed by Cal Fire, by a relative of my neighbors. We have no information as of yet on Grams' house. I give her a little smile, and turn to walk down the hall toward the room I'm using. I sit down on the bed, both unable to breathe and breathing frantically at the same time. I will have to tell the boys. I begin to shake, hard and relentless. I can't tell them yet. Not yet. I fight for air, but all I can suck in is pain, thick and heavy in my lungs.

How can I tell my kids about this? Our house is our haven. Each room has been reinvented to reflect a mother's love and the unique personality of each person. My boys have Minecraft themes, with red blankets and blocks and fireplaces with "diamonds" in them. Rocket ships we made hang from the ceilings, and they have vast collections on display from all of our travels of crystals, rocks, and minerals. Our living room is like a retreat, with a fountain and comfy furniture perfect for cuddling. Our dining room table is a massive piece, hand hammered Sheesham wood, with a long bench along one side. It barely fits the space. The hammered grooves of the worn table hold memories of art projects, Christmases, love. Glitter, paint, and scars bless the indentations of the wood. This is our special place, where the boys took their first steps, where we put up the Christmas tree every year, where we laugh and dance and cook and tickle and hide and seek and cuddle. This is our home. *Was*. Was our home. And I have to look into their little faces and tell them it is all gone. All of it, just...gone.

    I decide I need a night to process the loss, to grieve it briefly, and regain some strength before I talk to the boys. I just need some time to calm down and approach it fresh tomorrow. I can't do it tonight. I can't be strong in this moment, and that is okay. I give myself permission to experience the loss in my own time, in my own way, in my own head. This situation calls for flannel pajamas and any amount of sleep I can glean from the night hours. The shock protects me for now, and I am able to sleep from the exhaustion and the not yet knowing what the reality of all of this is actually going to feel like, going to be like. I will tell them tomorrow.

Chapter 15

God promises to make something good out of the storms that bring devastation to your life.

Romans 8:28

People advise me the next morning that I don't have to tell the boys right away. "It can wait. They don't need to know yet. Do you have to tell them? Can't it wait? Maybe you should wait." I respectfully disregard the suggestions. My kids deserve the truth, and need time to begin to process that truth. It doesn't feel right to prolong the grief progression. Eventually they will have to know, there is no hiding the fact that we are now going to be homeless, all of our possessions gone. So I opt for sooner rather than later. Better they hear it from me than overhearing an adult conversation, or seeing the map on the news. It needs to come from me, with me, with all of us together. *Us. We still have us.*

    The late morning light filters in through the blinds, dimmed by the thick smoke that hangs heavy in the air. The blinds cast a patterned shadow into the room, but all my mind can focus on is the conversation I am about to have with my children. The lights of my life, my two reasons why, the people I want most to protect in this life. I can't protect them from everything, and it pains me to know this is going to hurt them. I take a slow, deep, steadying breath. *God, please give me the words and the strength I need for this. Help me to comfort them.* This is not going to be easy.

    "Okay guys, family meeting," I call out, standing near the couch. I give them a minute to shuffle in and sit down. I sit down between them. They look at me expectantly, knowing that our family meetings are something to be taken seriously.

"I have sad news…," I pause for the briefest of moments. Then, voice trembling, I rip off the band aid. "We lost the house. I'm so sorry."

Andy nods. "I knew when we were driving out that it wasn't going to make it. I'd actually be more shocked if it had survived." He is thinking this through with logic, and not yet fully understanding what some of the repercussions are of losing your home, your community, and daily life as you know it. "I'm just glad we made it out alive." And this part, this truth, our truth, helps in dealing with the loss. We came so very close to losing much, much, more. But Tommy's truth is different. His experience wasn't ours. He doesn't process things by way of logic, he processes with empathy and emotions, one of his biggest gifts. And he is still so young.

"But Mommy, did you save my big bear?" His wide, hazel eyes are filled with tears. I swallow back the pain I feel for him.

"No, baby, I'm so sorry." I hug him tight, wanting to take it all away for him. I can't. I can't make it right. But I am here to make it better, to share perspectives, to comfort and guide. I am here.

"Why?" he wants to know, wants to understand all that he didn't experience with having to evacuate so quickly.

"There was no time to save all of our stuff, honey. Andy grabbed Froggie and that's it. A six foot bear was much too big to pack with us," I try to explain, but it all sounds pathetic. Words really won't ease the pain at this point.

"But, all of my favorite things are there. All of my stuff is there," he shares, beginning to comprehend the enormity of the situation. His home is there. But it isn't there. Not anymore. He begins to cry, but not a normal cry. This is a gut wrenching sound, a wailing siren of pure grief, a pain he hasn't experienced before. It's a howling, guttural force that I know is the sound of his little heart breaking. *My heart breaks with his*. My heart nearly tears apart for his sadness, for his loss. It's a physical ache in my chest, my body, my soul. I hold him tighter, and Andy moves in nearer, quiet but solid. He stands right next to me, like the little buttresses on huge pillars in ancient cathedrals. If you don't know to look for them you might miss the strength they add to the structure. I pull Tommy onto me and we lean into Andy. He leans in to us, reinforcing my body as I hold Tommy tight.

"It's going to be okay," I reassure him, whispering near his ear.

"No, it isn't. It isn't okay." He clings desperately to me, his mournful wailing almost unbearable to hear. I give him some time to let it out, to grieve, to honor the pain he feels. And then I work to calm him down, to reinforce that he is not alone in this.

"Hey, look at me. Look up at me Tommy," I whisper to him. It takes a while and a few more attempts, but finally, he looks up. I look from him to Andy, and back at Tommy. I take his precious face in my hands. "We got this." He starts to shake his head and looks away, but I gently hug his face with my palms. "Tommy, look at me," I repeat. I circle my hand around, between the three of us. "We got this," I tell him, emphatically this time. I glance at Andy again, and he gives me the briefest of nods.

"Okay Mommy," Tommy resigns. Even at his age, he knows we will tackle this together, knows that he is not alone in the grief, in the experience, in the situation. He knows that I will hold him for as long as it takes, knows that Andy will let him cuddle up next to him for comfort, knows that we will pray together through it. We stay like that for a long time, Tommy on my lap grieving, his head tucked into me, and Andy leaning against my side.

In the days that follow, my mind unforgivingly flashes on things we have lost. Everyone says it, even I have said it: "They are just things. Things can be replaced. People cannot." But here's the deal. That baby handprint can't be replaced. My great grandmother's Christmas ornaments can't be replaced. The special recipe of a Mother's love that Andy wrote out for me in first grade that was framed and resting on my kitchen counter by the toaster to read every single day can't be replaced. The comfort and security of being in your own space, your own bed, your home, can't be replaced. The hard wood floors where both my kids first walked can't be replaced. The paper hearts colored by the boys that were taped up all over my room to help speed up my recovery can't be replaced. The shadow box with anything shaped like a heart that Tommy found for me (rocks, beach glass, the inside of a black walnut shell) can't be replaced. The Lego heart that Tommy made when my grandfather passed away, his stuffed animal collection, favorite clothes, cherished crystals and handmade cards can't be replaced. The scarred old wooden chess board that Andy and I learned to play on can't be replaced. The familiarity of the house you grew up in can't be replaced. Our table, with the hours and years of love marked all over it, can't be replaced. And the reminders of that are constant, everywhere, each and every day.

    The reminders are fiercest at the shelters, because we have to begin to gather items that were lost. People donate just about everything, but I have no place to store any of it. I see dishes, toasters, pans, towels, and comforters. We just don't have anywhere to keep any of it. I take only what we can pack around with us, only the necessities. Even all of the storage units are taken, so we can't even collect stuff and keep it for when we have our own place. Who knows when that will be. Over fifty thousand people have been displaced, and there is just nowhere around here to accommodate us all.

    People at the shelter sites remind us to eat. Food trucks have brought in free sandwiches, coffee and tea, and salads. Water bottles and snacks are at every station, along with more breathing masks. I grab a hot tea, more for the comfort of the warm cup in my hands than anything else. I manage to snack on some almonds and take a granola bar to keep in my pocket for later. I have to eat to keep my body strong enough to make it walk around, digging through other people's things that we now need.

I leave, then immediately visit another shelter to get more clothing and come across a white knitted blanket. My mind flashes in an instant to the one that my grandmother made for me years and years ago. It was up in the loft, packed away safely with winter blankets and coats. *Damn.* I pick up the knitted blanket on the shelter table, knowing that it was made with just as much love and care. But it isn't the same, it's not from my Grams. It's not the same pineapple pattern, doesn't have my favorite tassels. It's too painful to look at right now, so I stuff it back into the pile on the table and turn away, blinking back the tears. It will be there for someone else, to comfort and warm someone who needs it. It isn't meant for me. Is any of this meant for me? This is so hard. How can I do this? *God, give me the strength to do this. Help me do this.*

I continue walking around, dazed, and literally walk right into a large storage container. I look down, my worn sneaker bumped up against a bin of Legos. I immediately picture the amazing battle bots that the boys have created over the years, the most prized ones left out on display and not to be dismantled. We constantly have building challenges at the huge table in the dining room, each of us getting a scoop of random Legos from the bin and having to use whatever pieces were in front of us to create vehicles. Then we "battle" them and see which design is the best. It all began with a lesson on the Apollo 13 hack; the boys hadn't yet heard about how the astronauts on that mission were saved. I explained the basics of what the astronauts and engineers faced that day, and tell the boys that they are now ready to build on their own, without the instruction manuals. I place a huge scoop of various Lego pieces in front of them, and say, "Sometimes in life, you have to work with only what you have in front of you. Now work together to build something with what you have." The Random Scoop Challenge is born, and we spend hours learning to design amazing creations with whatever haphazard pieces we get from the scoop.

I have to take my own advice in this situation now, have to apply the lessons I have taught the boys to my own actions. I look around the shelter, at the piles of clothes and toys and books and shampoo and used shoes lined up in rows on the ground. *Houston, we have a problem.* I have to take all of these random pieces, these fragmented gifts that have been placed before me, and begin to create a new life, a new experience for us. *Sometimes in life, you have to work with only what you have in front of you. Now work together to build something with what you have.* I have to get to work on this. I bow my head, humbled and grateful for what is in front of me. With renewed determination, I bend down to the tub of Legos, grab the handle on one side, and begin to drag it across the grass toward the parking lot. Today, we start over.

Chapter 16

I can do all this through him who gives me strength.

Philippians 4:13

I get to my car and pop open the back. The interior looks like a mini storage unit, and in reality, it is. Toilet paper, water bottles, pillows, blankets, and bags of clothes and toiletries fill up the third row seating area. All of the rental storage units in town and the close surrounding towns are filled with waitlists. I begin to rearrange, stacking precarious bags on top of each other, making space for the Lego bin. Future battle bots are a top priority. I shove everything in, defying both the law of gravity and whatever the law is requiring a sightline from the rearview mirror. The side mirrors and backup cam will have to do. And soon, we have to find a temporary place to stay.

Several of my colleagues have generously offered up rooms in their homes. Some people are purchasing RVs and trailers, parking them in bare lots and alongside homes. Every hotel room within a two hour driving radius is booked, filled with first responders, evacuee service members, and a minimal amount of fortunate refugees that were able to secure a room early on. Endless tents have been put up in fields near parking lots, especially near Walmart and churches. People are living in their cars if their cars survived. The shelters are absolutely packed. I just want a space that my kids can call temporary home through the holidays. Somewhere to have dinners, to have showers, to hang out. Somewhere that Santa can visit. Somewhere to preserve the traditions we have established. Somewhere to feel a bit grounded, to stabilize, recover. Everyone wants this.

I consider the multiple room offers from people that we know who live in Chico. After weighing all of the pros and cons, I decide on Ernie's place, with an owner that is a colleague, parent, and close to my age. It will likely be the easiest transition for everyone. Additionally, the house itself is in the safest zone as far as potential fires are concerned. His kids are rarely visiting, so there is plenty of space. When they do visit, briefly over holidays and summer, they will likely get along great with my boys as their ages are all close. It seems to be the best fit for us. My goal is to get in before Thanksgiving and begin to settle in through Christmas and the New Year. We need a few months, three at least, to get through the worst part of this. To get insurance claims filed and resolved, to begin to sleep through the night, to allow the PTSD to subside, to resume school and work, to re-establish routines in a new city. The best case scenario is three months, worst case six months. I hope. I talk to my colleague and explain how important it is that my boys don't get bounced from place to place any more. We need one place to be our temporary home base. We agree on three months, with a plan to reevaluate at that point, setting a goal of six months if possible. We agree to a fair rental amount to help us get back on our feet yet still contribute to the household expenses. My level of relief is indescribable. My boys will have a consistent place to stay. Santa can add us back onto his route. We can calm down a little and focus on healing.

I talk to the boys about this option, and tell them we will go over to the house and tour it, they will meet the owner and see how it goes. They agree that this is a good plan, and we head over there to take a look. The house is in a safe neighborhood, with sidewalks and cul de sacs. The backyard is fenced in with no points of escape for Harley. I look around and see no looming pine trees or any type of forestry that could threaten our safety. It all looks pretty harmless. It's perfect for what we need right now.

After the tour and spending a little time there, the boys agree that this is our best option. Though I can feel that it is awkward for them at first, and not our own space, I am optimistic that we will all adjust quickly. We don't have to stay in a cramped trailer or a tent, or one of the shelters. We will get to stay in a house, in a neighborhood. And we won't be staying with a complete stranger, we will be staying with a colleague, a father, someone who wants to help us through this. *Thank you.*

We move in our sparse belongings; a few pillows, a few clothes, a few toiletries. We don't have much but it's a start. Now that we have a place to put things besides in the back of the car, I can "shop" at the shelters for more clothing and creature comfort items. My main concern has been met; we have a place to stay and don't have to go from house to house, bed to bed, wondering what will be next. We can ground ourselves now, to begin the healing and rebuilding process. After Thanksgiving the schools will resume and the boys and I will be able to establish some type of normalcy in our routines. It is a start.

We stay three days, and though there are challenges, I do believe we can make this a sustainable situation until spring, possibly even summer if needed. Over fifty thousand people are displaced right now. The housing, schooling, and employment situations are a complete cluster. The smart move is to wait out the insanity. Things do settle down post disaster; you just have to wait for it. So I do what I do: plan to make the best of what we have.

Relatives come to town with donations, take us on trips to Target and Costco to get essentials. Friends and strangers arrive with gift cards and cash to help get us through and to purchase essentials. I get a blanket for each of us, snacks, socks, underwear, and two air purifiers because the smoke is still terrible. It has just been announced that this area is the unhealthiest place to be on the entire planet. The air quality is off the hazardous charts because of the fine particulates in the thick smoke. We all drive and walk around in N-95 face masks to filter out what we can. Cars are covered in dust and ash, refugees with wild hair and wilder eyes are everywhere. It looks like a low budget Sci-Fi flick or old episode of The Twilight Zone.

    I concentrate on only the essentials, and mostly for the boys. It is as if my focus can only be stretched so far. Basic needs first. They each have a jacket, two sets of clothes. We have to get bread, eggs, peanut butter, olive oil, and enough food for a few meals now that I have access to refrigerator storage. We each have a pillow, a blanket, and the boys have backpacks for school. And we have a tub of Legos waiting for all of our future inventions. I head to the grocery store to pick up the essentials, starting with food for breakfast tomorrow morning. I shop slowly at the closest store, all of the aisles unfamiliar. As I load up the cart, I hear a familiar voice behind me. It's a wonderful colleague and her daughter, who used to watch my boys when they were tiny. We give long hugs and smiles, catch up briefly, and they insist on paying for our groceries. Our meals are already blessed with love.

    I load up the car and go back to our new temporary residence, putting all of the grocery bags on the kitchen counter. The boys arrive, and sit at the island to have a snack. Our landlord, Ernie, arrives with his kids who are visiting for the upcoming Thanksgiving holiday, and calls my boys over to the kitchen table. I continue to unpack the groceries, fitting them into our designated spaces in the fridge and cabinets.

    "I think it would be good for all of us to establish some house rules," he tells them, opening up a laptop.

    "What about Mom?" Andy asks.

    "She's fine over there. Women can multi-task." I'm focused on my current chore, and although the comment rubs me the wrong way, I know his intentions are good and to be honest I am probably overly sensitive from exhaustion. I let it settle, and listen in as I finish unpacking the grocery bags. Some of the rules come from Ernie, some from all of the kids, because they all already know what house rules should be. But I wait this out, not wanting to sound snarky even though I kind of feel it.

1. No running around in the house
2. No making Harley bark
3. No rough housing with Harley
4. No jumping on furniture (It has already been openly shared with us that one of his kids has a challenge with this)
5. Knock before you enter
6. No Harley in the Master bedroom
7. Everybody contributes equally to cleaning the house
8. Clear or bus your own plate, cup, dish
9. No pulling or locking people out
10. If you want to borrow something, ask
11. No raging...If you need a break, take one
12. No interrupting
13. Eating should happen at the table or the island
14. If you have a problem bring it up. Or, call a meeting
15. No throwing Harley's toys in the living room or the kitchen

This is Ernie's suggestion, and at this one, I speak up. "We only have soft little toys for her that get tossed near to the floor. I'm certain nothing can break." She is such a small dog, and a puppy at that. She can't even carry a tennis ball in her mouth. I look around and actually don't even see anything that could be broken. No vases, no lamps, no fragile art. The place looks pretty minimalist and kid proof. Ernie remains adamant, repeating the rule.

"I don't really want to agree to not ever play with our dog here. We are very careful, and would obviously replace anything that ever got damaged. But I don't think anything here is at risk of that." He refuses to budge, so I finally say, "Okay, I don't like it, and even though we are renting it is ultimately your house." I glance at the boys and they know what this means. The list continues.

16. Ask permission
17. Explain things in a nice way
18. Try not to scream
19. Eat your own food, normally
20. Get permission from Mom to feed Harley
21. Try to be quiet in the morning and night

Ernie prints the list of rules, and posts it on the fridge. All four kids break from the table, and begin to play a peaceful game hide and seek. They all get along great, and the evening seems to be going well for them as they giggle and congratulate each other on genius hiding spaces. I take some time to think over the list making, and decide to chat with Ernie about it. We sit down and I explain my perspective.

"Next time, I'd like it if you and I can briefly go over things first as adults before we bring the kids into a discussion."

He interrupts, justifying that I was standing right there.

"Yes, multi-tasking, I remember. About that, it actually felt like more of a dismissal than a compliment. Regardless of how it was meant, I am very careful that my boys learn to see women respected. So from this point forward, I will be present and sitting down with them during any planned conversations. I need to consider their perspective, which is that they are not used to some unknown man taking over. I get that this is your house, but those are my boys, and I will be the one to lead, or co-lead, any meetings that involve them. It would also be nice to have a heads up ahead of time if we all need to sit down together, and I will make sure I'm not having to multi-task, but instead giving it my full attention."

"You should have come over or spoken up right then if that bothered you," he tells me, sounding defensive. I stay calm and stick to my point.

"In hindsight, yes, and I will definitely work on responding immediately from this point on. I really just needed to process this in a calm manner before talking about it privately as adults."

There is a long silence and I wait it out.

"I didn't really consider those points of view and I will try harder with communication," he finally says.

"I will too," I reply. The conversation ends well, but in the back of mind a little red flag is gently waving at me. I don't have the strength to psychoanalyze Ernie right now, or myself for that matter, in this new and foreign situation. I am just too weary. I round up the boys and we go through the motions of our nighttime routine, washing and flossing and brushing. We hang out on the bed with Harley until it is time for cuddles and prayers and sleep. Everything else will have to wait until tomorrow.

Tomorrow comes and goes without incident and we are now at mid-week, just before Thanksgiving. I'm not in a space to cook a full meal, certainly not in a space to roast a stuffed bird. This holiday for us will be just like the other evenings this week. Full of gratitude and time as a family. I make a list and head to the grocery store and grab the basics for soup. It will be the first meal I have prepared for us. I am exhausted, beat down, and grieving. But I can't wait to be fixing food for my boys. What a blessing.

The boys won't be home for a few more hours, giving me time to unpack the groceries and prepare the soup to let it simmer. I am so grateful to be doing this, so happy to be providing for my kids on this level. I chop, stir, season, and taste. I seriously make the best chicken soup. This soup doesn't stand a chance. Laundry is going in the drier; a load of some towels and washcloths that were at the donation center. The beds are made, and I have groceries for breakfast in the morning. Everyone has toothbrushes, soap, and a book to read tonight. *We got this*. I am testing the soup again as my new roommate/landlord walks in and drops a bomb of epic proportions, shaking the little world I have just tried to create for us.

Chapter 17

Bear with each other and forgive one another if any of you has a grievance against someone. Forgive as the Lord forgave you.

Colossians 3:13

Ernie holds the unsigned lease agreement in his hand and begins to aggressively explain that the amount we had agreed upon for rent isn't going to work. There has apparently been a huge misunderstanding as to both the length of time and amount of money we had agreed upon. I do not know how our agreement can now be clouded in confusion, but it is. He explains via yelling that the rent will now be over one thousand dollars a month more than our agreed upon amount. The total is way beyond what I can possibly afford, is more than my former mortgage, insurance, and taxes combined. A mortgage that I still have to continue paying until the insurance is settled. Dual payments are not an option for me if the rent will be that high. I'm not buying this house from Ernie, just renting some space here for a bit. While he continues to live here as well. But it isn't even the discussion about the absurd amount of money that concerns me. It is about the atrocious communication style I am observing. I am incredulous but remain calm. He works himself into a frenzied rant and then begins yelling that the new amount is what is "equitable."

Equitable because now people are desperate and will pay thousands over what is reasonable because they need a place for their children to live? Equitable because someone else can undoubtedly pay more than I can? Equitable because he has changed his mind now? Equitable how? I don't ask any of these questions out loud. I refrain because I will not engage in a conversation with anyone acting belligerent. Not unless I am conducting a suicide intervention. I tell my kids all the time to just walk away if someone is raging. Walk away, don't engage, don't let the situation escalate if someone is behaving irrationally. *We don't do crazy.* I turn and leave the conversation, tuning out the strain of maladaptive thought processes he is verbalizing, and I walk away.

In my room, I shake. I am furious, I am afraid, I am shocked, I am traumatized all over again. This is exactly what I wanted to avoid, and Ernie knows that. All I wanted was to avoid setting up a false sense of security for my kids. Now what? I think over the offers of places to stay. Should we live with the little league coach who is trying to quit drinking and his two boys? Four boys and a dog total? Or move in with the retired bachelor professor who is used to peace and quiet? Or, perhaps we live with the older Psychiatrist who wants to date me and is allergic to dogs and children? Do we keep staying with my ex-husband, his mother, and his girlfriend? Oy vey. My car as a shelter is suddenly very appealing. I mentally assess whether or not the three of us could actually sleep in it with the seats down. There really isn't enough room. Damn, damn, damn. I pick up my phone, praying that this isn't going to turn into a bad game of Russian roulette. We need a good space, an empty chamber. I can't handle one more bullet to the heart.

I scroll down through the names on my phone and hit the call button. Someone picks up the phone after a couple of rings. *Thank God.*

"Hey Dan. Is that offer of a place for us to stay still on the table?" I practically sob out the question. Amazingly, he is able to decipher my gibberish. He also seems immune to my imminent hysteria, which is a very rare but powerful occurrence.

"It is, yes, no one else is staying here. I did have a couple using the travel trailer parked on the street, but they have found other accommodations."

"Can you come get me please? Can I come see the house, come talk to you?"

"Of course. Send me the address." We hang up, and with shaking hands I message him my current location. I grab a hoodie and my purse and leave the house, standing outside shivering or shaking and waiting the fifteen minutes in the dark for my ride to arrive. It is drizzling, the light kisses from heaven signaling that the fire will soon be contained, soon be out completely if the rains stay. The soft droplets cling to my hair, my glasses, my face. It is cleansing, refreshing, smelling like new life after endless days of smoke and gloom. I breathe it in, and it is beautiful; it is just too late. Too late to stop the fire, too late to undo the trauma, too late to allow us to go back home. The damage has occurred, with so many people in grief and loss and lost. If only it had rained sooner. If only a lot of things had been different. If only. I see headlights round the corner and head my way.

I waste no time getting in the car. We drive, mostly in a peaceful silence, heading across town in the darkness and rain. The wet black streets reflect the lights of the city. After fifteen minutes we arrive at the house and go inside for the grand tour. The place is spacious and aesthetic. Wide arches, cathedral ceilings, high windows. Unique art adorns the walls, oriental rugs the floors, retro furniture in each room. The bottom floor is like a mini art museum. Our voices echo slightly off the tile flooring as I share my current situation. He calmly listens, empathetic, understanding. A stable force in the chaos that surrounds me.

He has a peaceful life, a good retirement, a gallery of a home, and a sanctuary of a yard. He can have his morning coffee surrounded by a state of serenity. The ambient sound of the waterfall in the backyard can be heard even inside the house. It's just so calm here. It's not like I can move in with two boys and a puppy and not be noticed. *You won't even know we are here.* Yeah, right. My boys are boisterous, loud, and high energy. We might drive him mad with the noise alone. Regardless, it's really the only viable choice we have.

He drives me back after we have made a plan. He will clear out part of the living space for us and we will be able to move in within a few days. I will stay tonight at the current house, and beginning tomorrow, the boys and I will stay with their dad until the new space for us is ready. I thank him profusely and we get back into the car, heading back out into the rainy night.

He pulls over to the curb and I walk into Ernie's house, the celebratory soup cooled and still in the pot on the stove. I pack it up into freezer containers without eating any of it. I have no appetite at all. I just want to be out of here. I clean up the soup pot and utensils, methodically washing, drying, putting away. I grab the laundry out of the drier and drag it into my room, folding it and packing it directly into a cardboard box. Tomorrow we move out.

My sleep is restless, knowing that tomorrow I have to tell the boys that we will be transitioning yet again to another house. And now, I have actually accrued some belongings for all of us, so I will also be packing and then moving. I think back to the NPR interview that was recorded yesterday morning. I was so happy to report that we had a place to stay, had found temporary housing and what I thought was a bit of security for us amongst the aftermath. It will air tomorrow morning, on Thanksgiving day. It was a good interview and focused on the positive. It's important for me, for all of us, to keep in mind that this is just another challenge, just part of the process. There is still so very much to be thankful for.

Thanksgiving morning is crisp and clear, the rain having beaten down all of the smoke. Finally everyone has freed their faces of the white breathing masks with the yellow elastic bands. Finally full expressions are now visible instead of just the tormented eyes showing. Children can be outside, there is no more house arrest. Once schools resume, recess will be allowed. Physical activities can now resume. Bike rides, walks, gardening. The fire is out. People everywhere are grateful. I leave the boys with their dad and promise to be back in time for an afternoon Thanksgiving meal. My drive back to Ernie's house is one of solemn determination. Just get it done.

    I pack up our clothing, blankets, pillows, toiletries, bath items, groceries, books, and toys. Backpacks, jackets, Legos bin, air purifiers, bread, eggs, pickles, dog bed, a case of toilet paper, laundry detergent, pajamas, shampoo, a box of clothes being saved for my Grams. It takes three trips. I lug everything from the first run up the stairs into the new place, turn right around, and go back for another load. Once I am on the last load, and back in my car ready to never come back, I remember the house rules posted on the fridge. I put the car back into park, run back into the kitchen, and pull it out from under the magnet. I carry it with me, not bothering to read it over again. I put it down on the floor of the passenger side of the car, keeping it safe until the boys and I can light it on fire and watch it burn.

Chapter 18

Come to me, all you who are weary and burdened, and I will give you rest.

Matthew 11:28

The moving is all done, and I'm so tired and weary. We have stayed at five different places in a matter of weeks. Now it will be six. Tomorrow the boys and I will move in to yet another house, move forward a little more. Confucius says, "It does not matter how slowly you go as long as you do not stop." I'm not stopping, but I am slowing down, my ass dragging like every day is Monday. Left foot, right foot.

And here is the thing. There are days I don't want to drag myself and the boys out of bed. There are mornings that I just want to stay in the warm blankets, cuddling with my two greatest loves, and let the day and the outside world pass us by without touching us. To just stay cocooned in love and peace and surrealism. But I get us up anyway. I adult, I face Monday, I make the phone calls and fill out the paperwork and show up for the appointments and do the shopping and pay the bills and teach the classes and cook the meals and parent my kids and do the laundry and remind the boys to floss and train the puppy and...I do all of it. I don't always want to, but I do it anyway. Sometimes you just have to do it anyway.

People ask me how. How do you do it? And here is the honest answer: *I do it with gratitude*. It is the antidote to anything negative. When my perspective reflects that I am grateful to get to do all of these things, honored to know and parent my amazing kids, blessed to be able to move around and be alive, they all become precious moments. Even the difficult ones. Sometimes, especially the difficult ones. Each moment here, each act, a blessing. I embrace that I survived that brutal illness, embrace that Andy and I survived the fire. *I am grateful.* This is what allows me the opportunity to keep inching forward, to rebuild our lives and to push through the setbacks. And there are always going to be setbacks. No one ever makes a perfectly steady climb up to the top after hitting rock bottom. We fall, we stumble, we have to rest, we almost lose hope, we wonder why it is so hard, we wonder if it is worth it. Every person has these struggles. Every single one of us. Yet despite the struggles, or maybe because of them, I know that I am pushing through for a reason. For many reasons. There are reasons for me to be here, things I want to do and share and give.

Each of us has a choice, a powerful and life altering choice, regarding what we spend our energy on. This brings to mind the first meal I ate at a restaurant after evacuating and learning that we lost the house. I gather with a few family members and a few new friends. We all sit down at Grana, a few small tables pushed together into one, with many small plates pervading the surfaces. The restaurant vibe is urban and hip, but it is quiet right now, between lunch and dinner crowds. The food is all beautiful, like little works of art mounted on circular, porcelain frames. I force myself to eat despite my appetite being so dismal. I can't fully enjoy the taste of anything through the grief. I want to return here after I've healed, to get to appreciate the quality of the meal. A friend of my cousin's sits down across from me, introducing herself. She then reaches over and takes my hands, squeezing them.

"I hear of your story on the Facebook," she says with a fantastic accent. "How is it possible? I am so afraid reading this. How is it that you are not under a table somewhere, just huddled under a table to not come out from fear?"

I think about this, because it is a legitimate question. We were traumatized for sure. Nearly died in a horrific nightmare of a scenario. With my child. Why aren't I under a table? My response is unapologetically honest.

"Because I choose not to huddle under the table. It is a choice, an effort. I will not spend my time in fear, letting that fear drive my life. I choose differently." This doesn't mean it is easy. It doesn't mean I always like it or that fears don't impact me. They do, and often. But I make choices every single day, throughout each day, that determine my outlook and state of mind. I choose. Not what occurs, or what each day brings my way, but how I respond to it. This is empowerment, how we can gain happiness and contentment. Choose how to respond, in your mind, to others, to yourself. *Think it over and then choose.*

She stares at me, her big brown eyes taking it all in. She can tell that I have spoken my truth.

"You choose," she repeats, slowly.

"Yes, I choose. I choose to get out of bed, choose to be an example for my kids, choose to still fight off the residual symptoms of that illness, choose to find a way to become a counselor." We all have pain and grief and difficulties. Every person in his or her own way. I want my challenges to benefit others. My illness will make me a better counselor, and now, so will the fire. I survived both for a reason. God still has plans for me here; I still have plans for me here. This is worth fighting for, worth pushing through pain and fear. A little bit at a time.

"It's too much, too big," she states. It is. It's too much to fathom. Getting through PTSD, being homeless, rebuilding entire communities, an entire city. Starting over somewhere new. Grieving the losses. I think about the age old question that I use to teach my students about conquering something ominous, something overwhelming. We go over it each term.

"How do you eat an elephant?" I ask them. All of the faces look back at me, considering. Some of the responses are humorous. No, you don't grill it. No, not with a side of fries. But it gets everyone thinking and puts a really simple perspective on our often complicated situations.

"One bite at a time," I tell them. Little bits, one piece at a time, which eventually add up to getting through it. If you just focus on that one piece, it's not as overwhelming. Pick one piece to work on next, and focus on that. Then on to the next piece. The next step. Little steps get you across the bridge too. Just keep going, a little at a time. Here, sitting at this restaurant, I try to finish my soup, one sip at a time. I get through half of it.

There are many things that keep me going in the weeks that follow. My boys, my students, my faith. These are all powerful motivating factors. What I am not expecting is the overwhelming support of colleagues, friends, coaches, principals, moms of the boys' classmates, and strangers from all over the world. I post our story on Facebook, and a highly respected friend suggests that I make it public, for anyone to access. He tells me people need to read it. Typically I restrict social media posts to within my close friends and family members, but this is a powerful experience. I take his advice and open it up to the public.

The responses are one of the most moving influences in my life, something I will never forget. Love, blessings, and prayers begin to pour in from everywhere, from all over the country, then all over the world. Love from Montana. Prayers for your boys from Mexico. Our hearts are with you from Texas. Praying for you all. Prayers from New York. We donated to your fundraiser from Wisconsin. May God bless you and your boys. Much love from India. Tears roll down my face as I read the thousands of comments that people share. Most of them from complete strangers that I will never have the privilege of meeting in person, never get to properly thank. Their words lift my broken heart, heal me with knowing that my community, my support group, now spans the entire freaking globe. I am humbled, filled with love, and most of all, so very thankful for each and every one.

Local people begin to organize. Food shows up, more cash is delivered, more gift cards arrive. People bring us clothing, pet supplies, detergent, makeup, pajamas, socks, school supplies, shoes. Others come and pick up what clothes don't fit and take them to the donation centers for us. Dinners are prepped, groceries are picked up, work reminders are made about deadlines and paperwork. And then, the Paradise Adopt a Family site is launched on Facebook.

People all over the country come together to assist families with specific issues that need to be addressed. A broken down car, a vet bill, basic supplies, a place to live, relocating, storage, help finding missing loved ones. We get selected for help, and Andy gets a desperately needed pair of shoes. Tablets are replaced, Rubik's cubes arrive, early Christmas and birthday gifts are sent. A young girl learns that Tommy's accumulation of Beanie Boo's was lost and sends him part of her own personal collection. He arranges them all around his pillow, their soft little faces with big glitter eyes peering over him. For the first time since the fire he is finally able to sleep through the night.

A former colleague and wonder woman calls me to see how the boys and I are doing. She asks if we need a trailer, would we have somewhere to put one? I explain that we are better off in Chico, close to the schools and the boys' classmates. But my Grams is going to need a place to stay. She is almost 90 and lost her home. She desperately wants a small space of her own. Of our entire family in this area, my mom's house is the only one left standing, and it is a twelve hundred square foot cottage with one bathroom. There isn't enough room to go around. But she has property that can easily host trailers. I share this with my dear friend, and she gets to work on passing along our information to some people she knows.

We don't hear anything for weeks, but I don't really think on it. I don't have time or energy to think on it. We are so consumed with just surviving right now. I am tired, I am weary, and I am going through the motions of it all with what little strength I have. Days and weeks blur into the next. I continue to trudge forward. Then I get a phone call, a call that will mark the beginning of a new path for me, for my boys, for us. Change is happening, and old prayers are now being answered.

Chapter 19

For God so loved the world that he gave his one and only Son,
that whoever believes in him shall not perish
but have eternal life.

John 3:16

I currently teach at a local Community College and nearest State University. I love what I do as a teacher, and I love how great each group of students is that I have the privilege to work with each term. After the fire, both campuses reached out to me with offers to have substitutes cover all of my classes. It was a generous, considerate offer. They all knew I had lost the house, was without a residence, and had the boys to care for. But I could not leave my students hanging to get through such a rough semester without me. This experience was a teachable moment, both for my students and for my boys to see, and no way was I missing out on that opportunity. I put on my big girl panties, the low rise jeans, surfer hoodie, and my sneakers and I showed up to teach.

Previously, I had worked for one year doing crisis counseling, finished my practicum requirements for grad school, and then got sidelined by long term illness, nerve damage, and various other side effects from the strong prescription medications. After the first year of medical leave, I still wasn't released to return to work. So I painstakingly finished my degree, doing the army crawl through the last year of licensure courses required by the state of California. It was an arduous battle, I fought with valor, and I won. I earned every single little piece of that Summa Cum Laude diploma. I did it for my boys, did it for me.

I'm proud of that accomplishment, proud of what it represents. It symbolizes not giving up, accepting support, working as a family, sacrificing, delayed gratification, pushing through despite adversity, setting an example. Yet I am still not using my degree in the way that I intended. Aren't I supposed to be counseling people? Aren't I supposed to be doing more suicide interventions? Helping students navigate struggles, crises, and educational challenges? I continue to fight for what I believe is right for our students, right for our college, and right for me, but no doors open up for a counseling gig. I try for an internship, a part time position, anything at our college's crisis center that will put me in front of students in need. I have meetings, make phone calls, have more meetings. I submit an application and interview for the counseling and advising department. I make it into the hiring pool but am not offered a position. I am put on the backup list and continue to wait. One year passes.

I come to terms, temporarily at least, with the fact that the doors to counseling are not opening for me right now. I don't understand it, but I put away my fighting gear and tell God that I did what I could on my end. Now I pray for him to continue to direct my path. The path ends up being teaching, which I am better at than I thought I would be, considering that none of my training was preparing me to teach in a classroom setting. I put my best efforts into it, though, and it is resulting in positive impacts for students. The classes I teach are on how to be successful in college and in life. I impart life skills, wisdom, awareness, and coping techniques to young adults. It is much more powerful than I first thought, more impactful than I first hoped. But in the back of my mind it feels like there is still something not quite complete, something additional I am supposed to be doing. I keep waiting for it to surface.

It is now the beginnings of December, and I wrap up my evening class at the University, taking the many stairs down to the ground floor. The old brick building smells like

1960 inside the cement stairwell, stuffy and musty from decades of trapped air. I push open the cold metal and glass door and step out into the brisk, dark, rainy night. I trudge through puddles, wet leaves, and muddy grass toward my car. I don't have a hood on my jacket or an umbrella yet, so my hair and glasses get wet, but I don't mind it. As long as I'm not on bed rest or outrunning a wildfire I don't seem to mind much when it comes to inconveniences or frustrations. I reach my car and toss in my backpack, shake off my coat, and throw in my snack bag. My vision is impaired by the wet glasses, so I search for something to wipe them down with as my voicemail messages play across the Bluetooth speaker.

The female voice I hear is familiar, soft and calm. It is the head of the counseling department at the community college where I teach. A few counseling hours are available for the upcoming Spring term if I am interested in joining the team. I can keep my teaching schedule and counsel around that. I go through the work schedule in my mind. There will only be one day per week that I can't pick up the boys from school. I suck in a deep breath and replay the message one more time before calling her back. It doesn't miss my attention that I struggled to get something just like this for over a year and within a month of letting go of it, of accepting that God has a plan in place, it is offered up to me. Just like that, I merely have to call and accept the position. I call her back, going over the details and answering some of her questions as I navigate the narrow streets near the University, trying to tamp down the giddiness and instead sound professional. I feel my heart lift and know that this little light, this glimmer of promise that the tides are changing in my favor, is what I have to focus on. I hold on tight to that little piece of hope.

I pick up the boys and we head back to the house, where I sit with them in the living room.

"Guys, remember that job I applied for last year?"

"The one you didn't get?" asks Tommy.

"That's the one," I say, grinning.

Andy chimes in, "You got it." He states it as a fact, not a question.

"I got it," I repeat, nodding. "For part of the time. And the other part is to keep teaching." Andy gives me a high five and says, "Good job."

"I knew you could do it Mommy!" Tommy gives me a tight hug. This is all the celebration I need. I don't need champagne or a steak dinner or to make phone calls. I just need these boys around me; I just need this dynamic of our little family. I just need us.

The season moves out of fall and into early winter as I finish up my classes for the term, grading final papers and posting final grades. The semester ends well despite so many students being impacted by the fire and subsequent shock waves of repercussions that follow disasters. Many families, many of my students, scatter near and far. Student housing is already being impacted by the demands of so many people needing homes. There is talk on campus of low enrollment for the following term because of relocation and predicted housing limitations. The price gouging will be equal opportunity and impacts all of us, even our local students.

Christmas nears, and brings with it miracles and exhaustion. I make calls to the Exooter scooter company to explain what happened to our former scooters. The company sends me three replacements for free off the showroom floor from Santa himself! People visit us at the house, bringing by bags of toys, clothes, household items, pajamas, gift cards, puppy treats, and helmets. The Christmas tree is crowded by the numerous gift bags falling all around it. It stands tall and lush, with only one string of lights gracing the branches. I just can't bear to hang up any ornaments. I can't deal with going out to buy some commercialized version of what we used to hang on our tree each year. It's too painful to face that all of our special ornaments are gone forever. Andy's blue baby bootie ornament, Tommy's wax candy cane from kindergarten, my great grandmother's antique candle clips.

The little ornaments with the boys' school pictures in them. A glass bell angel from my mom. The star topper that the boys take turns putting up each year. It hurts deep within my chest to even think about it. I am trying to keep our traditions in place as much as possible for the kids, but this, this I can't do right now. Not this year. I know I will lose it if I try.

And before we can blink, Christmas Eve is here, and I am relieved more than excited. It is sad to say, but it is the honest truth in my heart. During this most blessed part of the year, I am grateful but weary. We are all sick with a respiratory flu, all tired, all beaten down, again. Typically we would all be gathering at my mom's house for too much food, too much family drama, and all the love between us. Of all our family homes in Northern California, hers is the only one left standing. But this year is different, and she is still without water. Everyone has scattered for now, with my grams, aunts, uncle, and cousin leaving town to have places to stay. Even if we could all gather there, I wouldn't want to risk getting anyone else sick. This year, I just want the holidays to pass, to begin to move us into the year new and beyond. I go through another box of tissues and another bag of throat drops. 2018 can kiss my ass.

We go through the motions, each of us opening one Christmas Eve gift as a precursor to the insanity that will ensue tomorrow morning. It is always a mad rush of ripping paper, opening up plastic that has been adult-proofed, and fighting with security straps on the Nerf guns. Bows go flying, the dog frantically pawing at her stocking. It's a frenzy, and I usually love it. But this year we are all subdued. The boys don't want to write to Santa, don't want to make a wish list, don't want to go shopping, don't even want to collect more stuff that we have nowhere to put.

We clean up the wrap from each of our gifts, leave out cookies and milk for Santa and carrots for the reindeer. We drag our tired and sick bodies up the stairs and climb into the Queen sized bed. I lost my bible in the fire, so I pull up the story of baby Jesus on my phone and read it to the boys like I do every year. We go through it, and I explain it to them as we read, and let them explain to me what they understand as we go along through the verses. Then we say our nighttime prayers, each of us contributing our gratitude and wishes. We are crammed into the bed like sardines. Andy on the left, Tommy on the right, and Harley at the foot. On Tommy's side a chair is wedged up against the bed to form a small rail and prevent him from rolling out. I'm trapped in the blankets, paralyzed in between the boys. If I so much as sneeze, someone will fall out of bed. We rest, in between coughing fits and checking for fevers. Plugged noses result in major snoring most of the night. I wait for the boys to pass out and set an alarm on my phone for midnight just in case. I can't risk sleeping through. Santa still has to come tonight.

Around eleven, I drag myself out from under the boys and the dog, helping Santa and our elf, Melvin, to set up the scooters inside, along with a few other gifts. I shove pieces of tissue up my nose to keep it from running. I am shivering with a fever as I look around and survey the tree area. The room is packed with bags of donated gifts, the wrapping papers gleaming in the light of the tree. Some are labeled with names, but many are blank, mystery packages. I guess we will just open them up tomorrow and find their owners.

Somehow I make it back up the stairs, pry the boys apart, and squeeze in between them. The crack of dawn is going to be here way too soon. I rest my eyes, loving that I am here to hold these warm sweet bodies of my babes. The puppy turns around several times near my legs and burrows down. The boys fling their arms and legs onto me, nestling in their soft warm heads by my sides. It is the most precious Christmas gift I could ever want.

Then all too soon, it is morning, Christmas morning. The light blasts in through the bedroom window and we all struggle to find a position to block our eyes and go back to sleep. It is the first Christmas that doesn't have the boys up at dark with crazed demeanors. We are all sick. Our arms and heads are heavy, I can't sit up yet. My body weighs a thousand pounds. We hack and cough, sneeze and moan. It has to be the plague.

We lay in bed for another hour at least, just wanting to sleep so that we don't have to feel so miserable. We hold hands and I lead us through our Christmas morning prayer. Finally, we all decide to get up and go open gifts. It is a slow process and we all look terrible. Faces flushed with fever, hair beyond bedhead, eyes glassy, noses red and stuffy. This is a rough one. We head downstairs and sit around the tree. After each of us has a gift, we tear into them. I think it is more out of desperation to get it done than excitement this year. We are too sick to be enthusiastic like normal. We get through half of the gifts and everything from Santa. It's all we can do. We go back to bed and just lay there. Andy falls back asleep first, then me, then Tommy. Harley is content just to cuddle with us, already a protective and caring puppy. We rest a bit, welcoming sleep for our bodies, then get back up and go through the rest of the gifts and sort them into piles. House stuff, garbage, recycling, items to donate, toys and clothes to go upstairs for the kids. I'm relieved it is over. Next year will be better. It has to get better.

I spend the day slowly cleaning up the aftermath of our holiday held in someone else's house. It definitely doesn't feel like Christmas, but we are doing our best. I miss our worn out wooden floor, our soft, deep sofa, our kitchen table with marks of years past gracing the surface. I miss the state of normalcy that we all take for granted each day when walking into our home. I miss our stuff, our familiar little treasures and creature comforts, our space. And really it is that sense of home, the familiarity, everything that makes a house a family space that I miss the most. Our photos on the wall, the smell of our house, the belonging to a place that takes years to create. I miss our routines, the boys sitting in their rooms reading next to their fireplaces, throwing the ball down the hall for Harley, cuddling on the couch to watch movies, popping popcorn every weekend, leaving around laundry and dishes and miscellaneous crap wherever we want until we finally opt to clean it all up. I miss my favorite pajamas and the little art pieces the boys made through elementary school. I miss it all, and I know that even though the future has many blessings in store, it still won't be the same. It will never be the same.

Chapter 20

Serve one another in love.

Galatians 5:13

The hustle and bustle of Christmas passes, and yet the love and spirit of giving remain strong in this city. Local vendors and organizations continue to offer discounts and organize free item giveaways for survivors. Volunteers from all over continue to work long, arduous shifts. They roll into the FEMA site at the crack of dawn, and offer their time selflessly to try and make our lives a bit better. They look up information, help with paperwork, tolerate rude behavior, see lines and lines of people day after day, don't take lunch breaks or get up to use the restroom or stretch their stiff muscles; they carry in cases of water, snacks, stacks of applications, boxes of envelopes holding gift cards. The lines take hours and hours to get through, volunteers have spent hours and days and weeks and months doing the same thing in the same little cubby every single day. Over and over and over again. Calling out our endless numbers from the sign in sheets. *Number 296. Number 297. 297? Do we have 297? Last call for number 297. Number 298.* They see refugees who wear the face of grief, the look of loss, the expression of despair. Some of them need to shower. Some of them are angry. Many of them are ill. Most of them cry. And somehow, every single volunteer I see shares a smile, gives away hugs, and sends each person off with good wishes.

Part of the mall has been transformed into emergency services areas that follow a natural disaster of epic proportions. It is a one stop shop for all things related to recovery services after total devastation. At the front of the building there are traffic attendants assisting with parking which is insane. Thousands of people have to visit this site. They park and walk, and line up outside the building under canopies and stand in line, waiting to get in. Just inside the doors is a security guard. "Any guns, knives, things that can be used as weapons?" He asks it to every single person, having had to repeat it a billion times already. At hearing the question, some people are surprised, some are confused, some are smartasses. The guard remains calm and steady, allowing one person through at a time. From there, we wait in line to sign in. We show our ID, dig around for the FEMA registration number which should be memorized but no one can seem to bear committing it to long term memory files. It makes it too permanent, too impersonal. We want so much more out of life than being constantly identified by a FEMA number.

Eventually we pass check in and are given a map indicating where all the services are located. Each area is partitioned off and labeled. DMV, emergency medical services, mental health services, county records to replace birth certificates and social security cards, United Way, Red Cross, Tzu Chi Foundation, Small Business Administration, FEMA information, Cal Fire Organization. At each area are volunteers, bottled or canned waters, snacks, hand sanitizer, and sign in sheets.

During one visit I have Tommy with me, which I try to avoid but can't completely. The boys don't need to be here, don't need to see this. Or maybe they do. I often wonder what the future will hold for them, what will come of their having gone through this. It is shaping us, that much is clear. Into what, for exactly what, is still unknown. We move slowly through the fog of devastation on blind faith.

We wait in the next line, and Tommy gets hungry and thirsty. I grab him a Kind nut and chocolate bar from the bin on the table by Cal Fire, where we will be getting a gift card. I see cans of water and grab two. He pops it open and begins to drink, when I notice that it has the Anheuser Busch logo across one side. It says water on the other side, but it still looks wrong to see my young child with this can pressed to his face. I turn my can over and read the back label. The company that I know as Budweiser beer completely shuts down beer production to instead can filtered water to distribute to disaster sites just like this one. Well, that is really cool. I drink my water, thinking that even though I haven't had alcohol since my illness, I could probably use a cold Bud right now. Maybe they should donate beer along with the water. This is a lot to get through, that is for damn sure.

Refugees visit the FEMA site multiple times. There is only enough time to get through one or two services each visit. And once signed up on the list, there is no time to go get food or use the restroom and risk losing the precious place in line. We all sit and stand around, for the most part silent, just waiting it out. There isn't anything to say right now. We are all devastated, all lost, all exhausted and sad. Most people don't even make eye contact. The looks are just too difficult to take, I guess. When people do meet each other's eyes, the small grimacing smiles or brief nods are enough. None of us have to say what we are all thinking. *I know. Is this our reality? Us too. We feel it too. This really sucks. Hang in there. Praying for you. Praying to God for all of us.*

The days in line, the weeks of dealing with insurance calls and meetings, and the months of paperwork all take their toll. The shelters provide an ideal setting for illnesses to spread. It isn't too long before we all get word that the Norovirus has broken out and is spreading. This happened the year before when flooding and the risk of the Oroville dam breaking caused huge populations of evacuees to be crammed together in shelters. The boys and I volunteered at the fairgrounds, bringing in supplies for children. The next day the Norovirus was reported, but thankfully the boys didn't get it.

Our current stress levels are high, and it impacts our immune systems and we spend the next couple of months sick, back to back. There isn't a day that all of three of us are well at the same time. We take turns with flus, coughs, fevers, and for me, migraines. And when we get sick, we get hit hard. I don't know if it is the lack of immunity, the power of the mutated viruses, or our weak systems compromised from smoke poisoning and inhalation. Perhaps it is a brutal combination of all three. The dark circles under our eyes don't lift, purple and deep like a bruising of the soul around the eyes. We are all thin and pale. The boys snap at each other, and at times it takes all my restraint to not snap back. Somehow we keep going, keep getting through it. The New Year is almost here, almost giving off hope of a new beginning.

On most years, New Year's marks a time of celebration, of declaring resolutions and planning for the year ahead and all good intentions to stay on that diet, stay sober, keep hitting the gym, blah blah blah. For thousands of refugees, this year is not like other years. Many survivors want to ring in 2019 by giving 2018 the middle finger. I'm ready for a new start myself, though January itself won't be providing that in all the ways we want. I don't ring in the New Year with champagne and a kiss. I don't make any resolutions. I don't make any promises that I might not keep. I welcome closure of the calendar year, though recovery doesn't concern itself with days or months or years. I try my best to let myself be open to what the year might bring in between the realities of piecing back together our lives.

New Year's Eve this year is just like any other evening for me since the fire, and I snuggle into bed counting my blessings. It is more my typical gratitude practice than anything celebratory. I am able to rest briefly, happy to allow 2018 to pass us by and become history. I sleep, with no intention of staying up until midnight. Getting rest is much more important.

Then, suddenly, I wake up hearing the propane tanks exploding again. *Boom, boom, boom.* Oh no. Not again, not ever again. Where are we? What is happening? I run to the window, disoriented from sleep and adrenaline. I see nothing, no flames, no flashes, no threats. I keep staring out into the street, looking for fire, smelling for smoke. Nothing. Then it dawns on me as I hear the booms again. Firecrackers. New Years. Celebrations. Ugh. I return to bed but cannot sleep. Each crack and boom is like a time portal back onto that slab. Every cell in my body is alert to danger, awake with the possibility of fleeing.

I now understand why Veterans struggle so much with sounds. Why my dad hates hearing aids because every rustling leaf or snapping twig, every little sound, might be the enemy. Why my neighbor Gene can't relax at the ocean because the crashing waves sound like bombs. Why fireworks can trigger PTSD. You can get over it but you never, ever forget.

Chapter 21

When she speaks, her words are wise, and kindness is the rule for everything she says.

Proverbs 31:26

As the drunken shenanigans of New Year's participants wind down, the little street outside of our window quiets for the night. It takes a long time for my body to accept that there is no threat, there is no fire. After what feels like hours of listening to my audio book as a distraction, I finally feel my muscles relax and my mind settle down. When it does, I have one last thought before sleep consumes me. *Hallelujah, 2018 is over.*

2019 arrives, bringing with it a packed schedule of insurance paperwork, prepping for classes, homework for the boys, and all of the usual household operations required to get us through an average week. This morning, I'm visiting my mom and brother before work, having a cup of tea, when my cell phone rings. It is a man I've never met calling about the trailer for my Grandmother. It has been hauled up from Southern California and they want to deliver it tomorrow! I am stunned that this is actually happening for my sweet Grams. We briefly make the arrangements for the delivery, and I give him a shaky and tearful thank you. Complete strangers will be providing housing for my grandmother.

A little about my Grams: she is the sweetest, most caring person I have ever had the privilege to know. She never speaks negatively about anyone, and instead just prays for everyone. She is a true lady, and always has graciousness and doing the right thing in the forefront of all of her actions. She still has nearly black hair even into her late eighties, the big curls framing her fair face and green eyes. Pictures of her as a young woman put the likes of Lauren Bacall to shame. She could easily have been a Hollywood starlet, was even sought after by agents. She declined all offers. She preferred the simple life, the family life, the Christian life.

Because of her, my faith has expanded. She offers words of wisdom without imparting her opinions or judgments into the lives of others. I often go to her for references in the Bible, and she always knows where to find that particular verse or lesson, and can help to deepen my understanding of the scripture. She just knows how to explain it in a way that makes it easier to understand and is always willing to sit with me and go over questions and how to interpret the lessons.

Grams is extremely witty and has a dry sense of humor that can be missed if you don't pay attention. She loves with her whole entire heart. She deserves somewhere to be comfortable, especially after the loss of my grandfather last year. They were married for over seventy years. Can you even imagine? Even through his last year with us, he and Grams danced together in the kitchen on Sundays. Theirs is a love affair that still continues, even through death. She still talks to him, still holds his photograph for comfort, and still loves him fiercely.

The trailer arrives, slowly creaking up the long driveway, with angel volunteers on board who have made this all possible. It's absolutely perfect. We have them park and level it on a little knoll, overlooking the garden. They open up the pop outs, which make it larger than I had expected. The inside is immaculate even though it has been used before. Each little nook and cabinet is filled with utensils, soups, washcloths, a coffee pot, new linens, band aids, hot chocolate mix. The interior is done in my grandmother's colors; light blues and grays and greens. The towels and blankets are also just as she might pick out for herself. I add to it by leaving a collection of beautiful yarns, knitting needles, and crochet hooks that were donated to her. Divine intervention comes to mind immediately as I walk through it and inspect all of its little blessings. Grams will love it.

When she gets to see it, all of my expectations and hopes of her reaction are exceeded. She walks through with twinkling eyes, discovering the contents of each cabinet like a gift on Christmas day. She carefully takes out each item, left for her with love, and looks at them all in awe. She declares each item precious, sweet, perfect. I hear, "Oh my word," and "Isn't that something," and, "Just lovely." The glasses are perfect, the towels her favorite colors, the coffee pot adorable. She loves the tiny fridge and stove and sink. She cries happy tears and tells us that the Good Lord provides. Watching her and seeing this firsthand, I know that He does.

I also know that we live in difficult times. I know that we face evil in this world. I know that it can wear us down and desensitize us to the point that it makes it a challenge to keep caring so much. I see it every day. But this disaster has brought out the goodness in people, has rallied giving and loving and random acts of kindness from all over the globe. There is still so much good in the world, and it is important that we take time to notice it. It often gets buried under the drama and violence and fear. There are still people changing the world, there is still amazing grace being demonstrated, there are still relentless miracles happening all around us.

Chapter 22

For this child I have prayed and the Lord has granted the desires of my heart.

1 Samuel 1:27

I don't know if it is the exposure to smoke and all the particles it carries that compromises our immune systems or if it is the stress of grief and homelessness. Perhaps it is a wicked combination of the two. It could also be that the shelters are a breeding ground for viruses and disease, and the town just incurs higher illness rates as a result. Whatever the cause, Tommy gets ill and it is a beast of a virus. It begins as a respiratory bug, and takes over his body. His skin burns with a high fever. He never gets high fevers, it is always Andy. But not this time. His little body has goose bumps all over, he shivers, and his skin all over is crazy hot to the touch. I give him acetaminophen and wait for the temperature to drop. It doesn't. I scan his head every couple of minutes. 102.7. I strip him down to underwear. 103.2. I begin slathering a cool damp cloth over his hot skin. 103.2. He flinches and whimpers every time the cool cloth touches him. 104. 104.2. 104.6. It won't get down. It hits 105 and I am not taking any chances, so we make a trip to the ER.

I am highly allergic to anti-inflammatory medications, which unfortunately include aspirin and ibuprofen. I go into anaphylaxis with both, and because of this Tommy is on the waitlist to be tested for allergy to ibuprofen by his pediatrician in Paradise. There is no telling when that will be happening now. Andy is thankfully not allergic and can take it. With Tommy, it hasn't ever been an issue because he never gets high fevers. Until now. The nose swab they run comes back positive for the flu, Influenza A, a viral infection. His lungs are clear, his nose is clear, no signs of a secondary infection, no pneumonia present. The nurse explains that they are seeing large caseloads of patients in the hospital for this particular flu; it's a powerful viral strain and the flu shot did not immunize people against it. It is taking about ten days to run its course. I can't imagine eight more days of this for my kid.

The doctor on call makes it to our room quickly and determines that it is worth the allergy risk to administer ibuprofen and watch Tommy in the hospital for any reactions. They have to get the fever down. It's been too high for too long. The nurse preps the little medicine cup with the dosage based on weight and hands it over to Tommy. He refuses to drink it, refuses to even try it. They struggle with every type of reasoning possible and finally the nurse turns to me.

"Okay Mom, you need to get him to do this or we will set up an IV tube. Doing it that way, he gets the full dose all at once and any potential reactions will be impacted by that. I'll give you a few minutes to convince him." She steps out of the room, leaving me with the task of getting my sick kid to drink something that may cause anaphylaxis. I stare at the tiny cup of pink liquid and all the fears swirling within it. Will his face and throat swell? Will he be able to breathe? Will he need an epipen shot? I take a breath and begin to talk myself down off the ledge before I can look at him. Many people are not allergic. Andy can take it. We have to get the fever down. We are in a hospital where they can treat a reaction.

I explain the dangers of high fever to him the best that I can, which does no good. Finally I tell him the bottom line; him he can either drink some of it slowly and watch for a reaction or they can inject it into his IV all at once. He understands and takes a sip. We chase it with apple juice. We do this fifty times. Sip, wince, apple juice, prayer. We make progress with the little cup of what I hope isn't poisoning my kid.

The nurse sits with us and times him for any adverse side effects. I stand by his bed, holding his hand. I pray, hard. Not just a routine thank you for our blessings type of prayer. This is my baby. I pray the prayers of a mother needing her son to be okay. Three minutes pass like hours. Five minutes pass, then ten. Twenty. Thirty. Forty five. He is fine. No hives, no rash, no swelling lips or breathing problems. The fever begins to drop. *Thank you God*. I can breathe again. They keep us for a while longer, to observe his vitals. Everything looks good.

They direct me with instructions to stagger Tylenol and Motrin and how to track the timing of each one both separately and concurrently. They tell me to watch his fever closely, which is still hovering around 103. We are cleared to leave with strict instructions to return if anything unusual occurs or if the fever peaks again and won't come down. However, they don't expect us to have to revisit the ER again today and neither do I. But I'm so wrong, they are so wrong, and we will be returning tonight.

I get Tommy back into bed and set an alarm for the next dose of medicine. We nap, but before the alarm goes off he stirs and I sit up, taking every waking moment to check his temperature and use the damp washcloth to cool him down. He sits up, looking around. For a moment, I wonder if he is about to vomit, because his expression is not right. But he doesn't vomit. It's much, much worse.

"Baby? Tommy? Are you okay?"

He looks toward me, but not fully at me. His eyes are not right. "Baby. Talk to Mommy. What's going on?" He stares, not responding. "Tommy." He looks past me. Eyes open, but not there. What the hell is happening? Febrile seizure? I check the clock again, timing it, trying to get him to respond. Two minutes? He should be speaking by now.

"Tommy, I need you to talk to me baby. Say something." He doesn't. I keep trying to elicit any type of response as I get up and make a plan. "What is two plus two?" He knows this from years ago, but I just want a response. He shrugs slowly and smiles, the face of lunacy on my child. I grab my cell phone. "What is your name?" He shrugs again, and I believe him. He doesn't know anything right now. He begins to climb toward the edge of the bed. "Wait, what are you doing?" I ask, stopping him.

"I'm going to climb that." His soft voice is full of awe. He points past me. I look, but there is just the wall. At least he is speaking now, but what he is saying is not a good sign.

"Climb what, baby? What do you see?" He points and begins to laugh. Not a normal laugh. A maniacal, crazy laugh. Is he hallucinating? I call 911. This is not okay.

"911, what's your emergency?" I quickly explain Tommy's fever, lack of responsiveness, and then describe what has occurred since.

"We will connect you with medical dispatch, one moment." They connect the call, and I have to give my name, phone number, and address. Where are we even living right now? I remember the address and even the cross street, thankfully. They go over Tommy's symptoms with me and send an ambulance out as we speak. They begin giving me directions. Secure any pets. Make sure the front door is unlocked. If he vomits, turn him on his side. If he loses consciousness..." I begin to shake. I run downstairs and flip open the deadbolt and turn on the porch light. I turn and fly up the stairs, making a new personal best time.

"Ma'am, are you fine disconnecting the call?" I'm not fine. My child is not fine. "No, I'm not. Just stay with me until the medics arrive." My voice wobbles.

"Yes, of course. I'm here on the line for you. How is his breathing?" I check it, and it's a little fast, but not unusual for having a fever. I gather up my phone charger, water bottle, and clothes for Tommy because he is still in underwear. I dump it all in my bag. I hear the wail of the ambulance approaching and thank the dispatcher profusely. The moral support and a voice on the other end of the line can make such a huge difference during an emergency.

We disconnect the call just as the EMTs open the front door and jog up the stairs. Two young women appear looking concerned, compassionate, and badass at the same time. They cram into the room with all the bags and gear hanging from their arms. They immediately assess the situation, talking to both Tommy and I while pulling out equipment to check vitals. Usually it is me being checked, not one of my boys. Both sides suck, but this side is indescribably worse. I'd trade him in a heartbeat.

It is quickly determined that we need to take him back to the ER. The ambulance is prepped and will give us a ride, contacting the hospital on the drive. We all go downstairs, crossing the cool dark night air toward our ride. The flashing ambulance lights are the only disruption in this otherwise peaceful cul de sac. The EMTs help Tommy onto the gurney, laying there strapped in with only his underwear and shorts on, and he looks so small and vulnerable then that my heart squeezes in pain and fear. Another EMT cracks open an ice pack and puts it under Tommy's neck to cool his body down.

We roll out of the driveway and into the street, and I clutch the metal hand bar near the ambulance bench as we rock back and forth, needing to stabilize my body and my mind. My other hand holds Tommy's little one, heat radiating off his palm and fingers from the fever. I answer questions about Tommy's symptoms, behaviors, normal diet, routine, medical history. Nothing in his past is indicative of this; no high fevers, no health problems, no reactions, nothing. Just a healthy young kid. The EMT makes notes on the blue rubber glove stretched onto his hand as we drive.

Tommy dozes in and out of sleep as we ride along, his little body strapped to the gurney as we rock side to side. I answer many questions about his health and symptoms with the eleven minutes taking seemingly forever. I mean, it's an ambulance, could we go a little faster?

Upon arrival they get us into a room right away, wheeling Tommy's gurney straight into the hallway from the ambulance. They pick up his sheet at both ends with him still lying on it, and easily hoist him onto a hospital bed. The bed weighs him and is operated with the slight touch of buttons at both the foot and head ends.

Staff shifts have changed, and now a different ER doctor is on call. I ask him about a possible reaction to the medications causing this behavior. He dismisses the idea immediately and attributes everything to the virus. I ask about febrile seizures. This is also dismissed, as Tommy is apparently out of the age group commonly affected by them. Okay, so two strikes against my theories, and nothing as of yet to explain the freaky behavior and unresponsiveness.

"So Doctor, what exactly do you think is the cause of the symptoms? He was staring but not seeing. Didn't answer me for several minutes. Then he didn't know who I was, didn't know who he was. He then thought there was something in the room to go climb and tried to walk off the bed. That's not normal." I go over it all again.

"It's likely the virus, the fever," he says, "Haven't you ever had a fever before?"

"I have, but not to the point of not responding. Or hallucinating. Or not knowing who I was." I remain barely polite and very assertive. I do not like this doctor. Have I ever had a fever? Seriously, does he ask all of the patient's parents that? What a jerk. Let me say this: I'm highly respectful of others in general. I respect that this doctor has been to med school, works the ER shifts, has probably seen more numerous cases than I care to know about. But no level of education, no important title, no income amount, can prevent one from being an utter jackass. And this guy here is case in point. I look at him, my eyebrows probably up into my hairline, waiting for some type of decent response.

"I see," he replies. See what? What does he see? My point? My attitude problem? My disappearing eyebrows?

More discussions between him, me, and the nurse occur. The fever is still high. They recommend another round of Motrin given the timeframe of the last doses. I'm reluctant but understand the need to take the fever down, especially if it was some type of febrile seizure despite what the Doctor disregards. They dose him and we all wait. Again, no hives or swelling, no rash, no breathing or heart rate problems. No allergy.

After the required several hours it always takes at emergency rooms, we finally get back home again and go back to bed, thinking we are in the clear of some freak occurrence now that the fever is slightly lower. Now we can get some rest, now we are less at risk for seizure, now we can put this nightmare behind us and I can just concentrate on nurturing my kid back to full health. Now I can lay back and breathe. Or so I think. How many times can I be wrong tonight?

The freaky symptoms recur, and by now I am determined to figure out what is causing my kid to be unresponsive and then hallucinate with delirium. I log in to my drugs.com account and run an interaction check for Acetaminophen and Ibuprofen. No interactions found. I dig deeper and Google it adding the word "child' to the search parameters. Scrolling down, I find that some research has been conducted on children and the rotation of ibuprofen and acetaminophen for fever reduction. Finally I discover a medical journal article abstract that sounds like what I am looking for. I log in to my medical journal database accounts and enter the DOI, which is a specific alphanumeric string assigned in order to find a particular article on the internet after publication. Jackpot.

Research shows that children, and specifically male children within Tommy's age range can severely react to a combination of ibuprofen and acetaminophen by experiencing delirium, hallucinations, unresponsiveness, coma, and death. The studies I find give descriptions of reactions just like

Tommy's and then some that are much, much worse. Thank God it didn't induce a coma, some of which in these cases can lead to death. My heart still hasn't settled down over this. I pull him even closer and give him lots of water to begin flushing out the medication, prayers humming through my body to the point of my chest aching. He needs to pull through this soon so that he can get by either with just acetaminophen or, ideally, no meds at all.

He sleeps in my arms as I sit propped up against pillows and the back of the bed, still wiping his forehead with the damp cloth. I doze off and on, waking often to check on him and keep his body cooled down. He whimpers as he sleeps, a heart wrenching sound of pain, and I immediately hope I can forget about it later. I talk softly to him, soothing words and prayers of love, heard even through his feverish sleep. At some point I fall into a deep sleep fueled by exhaustion and fear, still sitting up, my head hanging to the side. From far, far away I hear a soft groan and feel the bed slightly vibrating. With the little strength I have left, I lift my head from sleep and realize Tommy is shivering on me. I put my hands on him and feel that he is drenched in sweat, his clothing and the light sheet around us cold and wet. His hair is soaked and his entire body covered in goose bumps. As he shivers in my arms I feel a tear slide slowly down my cheek, shimmering full of the purest gratitude and relief. The fever is gone.

Chapter 23

Everyone should be quick to listen, slow to speak and slow to become angry.

James 1:19

I'm relatively young to have survived the things I've made it through so far. To date, these include near death from a virus and secondary infections, extensive nerve damage, long term illness, near death by wildfire, loss of home to fire, relocation, and the post fire list goes on and on. I had a rough childhood of poverty and an alcoholic father, struggled to put myself through college, and had a lifeless marriage and a just as lifeless divorce. And I don't find time to complain about any of it. I can use my past experiences to get through whatever else life presents in my path. I am a better counselor, better parent, better person for having been through it all. So when my son begins to enter puberty, I know I can handle it. At least, I think that I can.

I can honestly say that nothing has prepared me for the changes my sweet Andy is just beginning to present. And nothing has prepared me for how those changes are impacting our relationship. I have a degree in Clinical Psychology with an emphasis on crisis and trauma counseling. I have a strong faith grounded in Christianity. I am emotionally stable, logic, and realistic with a positive attitude. But puberty. Oh, my heart. Puberty is such an ugly beast at times. My sweet, caring, loving boy is beginning to act disinterested, defiant, disrespectful, and this is likely a mere glimpse of a whole heap of other behaviors yet to come that I won't even bother to list.

It's the first thing that I am angry about. Through this entire ordeal, I haven't really experienced any anger. I didn't have that emotion throughout my illness either. But this, these changes right now, the timing of it all gets me pretty mad. And here is the reasoning: My kid can't even experience this in his own space. Neither can Tommy or I for that matter. We are all blindly feeling our way through this in someone else's home, in someone else's space. There is no privacy, no familiarity, no normalcy.

The worst part of it is that I feel like precious time is being stolen away, again. We lost enough days throughout my illness, and we don't need to lose any more. While I am so grateful that Andy and I were both granted an extension on this life, I can't help but look back at these past five months and think about how this all could have been easier if we just had our home. It wouldn't all be a blur, wouldn't all just be about trying to survive and function and get through it. It would be different, better. But it's not.

Instead, there is constant bickering between the boys. These boys that used to be best friends and constant companions. Now the age difference is suddenly exponentially greater. Andy makes an art of smartassery, which Tommy doesn't understand yet. I get it, and even appreciate most of the humor behind it, but that doesn't make it appropriate behavior for his age. As cool as I am, my car is not the middle school playground. It's just not.

I roll up to Andy's school for drop off and he gathers up his backpack and next term's request for classes.

"See you after school, kiddo. Have a good day," I say to him as he is exiting the car.

"Not you," he says with a weird, scrunched up face and high voice as he shuts the door and walks away. I stare, mouth open, and analyze the face. Sarcasm? Joking, not joking? Sorry, not sorry? What the...? I contemplate parking at the curb and going after him right then and there, fantasizing about letting the natural consequences of a public maternal rant on campus manifest into an organic form of punishment. Maybe I could even get my hands on the loudspeaker and demand he visit the office to issue an apology. Maybe I will just seek revenge and volunteer to work the next dance, serving punch and pizza and hugs and making his pre-teen life equally tormented as a payback. I enjoy that fantasy for a moment, imagining it all playing out.

I sigh, telling myself to get a grip. He is going through so much, I tell myself. Let it go for now, and talk to him when the vein isn't popping out of your temple, I tell myself. I know this is the hormones, the stress, the way of prepubescent boys and their mothers. I know the psychology and the chemistry and the physiology of it all. But damn if it doesn't sting like hell. Eventually I recover from the shock, and slowly exit the drop off zone, getting immediately cut off by a young woman in a blue Volkswagen bug who doesn't honor the every other car rule. You know, where in congested areas of merging everyone takes turns? That one. My eye twitches, but I manage not to offer her sign language or expletives. I wave generously at the next person who understands the rules of the road and ushers me out with a quick motion. This puberty thing is going to be rough.

In the upcoming weeks Andy and I have several discussions that revolve around the difference between how parents should be treated versus friends. It is hard for Andy, perhaps because we always were so close, to now try and define what our new relationship will look like through puberty. He thinks that it is fun to roast and to tease, and as this is how all of his buddies relate, on one level I understand. But in my mind, the right thing for children is to have a parent, not another buddy. He is entering a volatile stage for males in particular, and even though he doesn't know it, he needs me to be consistent in my parenting, firm yet loving, accepting yet strict with the core values such as respect. I explain to him what types of comments are inappropriate or hurtful and should not be made toward adults, especially this one. It takes a little while for him to grasp the concept but through observing other parents and their children of the same age, he begins to see what is acceptable and what is not. He slowly begins to come around and mellow out. And in the back of my mind, I just know we need to get into our own space so that we can resume as a family independent of PTSD, a cramped living space, and someone else's house.

We try to have "normal" weekends as much as possible. The thing is, though, nothing is even close to normal post natural disaster. On this particular Sunday, Andy is having breakfast with his father. He gets picked up at 9:30 and runs out the door. "See you soon, kiddo!" I call out after him from the front steps. He waves but doesn't look back. I watch the car roll away, then head back in to hang out with Tommy. We cuddle in between getting organized for school and work tomorrow. I check the laundry, make sure my lesson plans are ready to go, and tidy up the bathroom. The weather is dreary, but I love it. Gray cloudy skies and intermittent rain, low temperature but not freezing. Not bone chilling cold, just a cool damp cleansing of the skies and the earth. I have the window to our room cracked just enough to hear and smell the rain. My phone rings, and it's not the normal ringtone. It's not a friend or a colleague or a solicitor. It's the boys' father, Ken.

Why is he calling so soon? Does Andy feel okay? Did he forget something? A thousand maternal questions race through my mind, synapses firing at the speed of light as I reach for the phone. I'm holding my breath but manage to say, "What's up?"

"Okay, they are here now checking Andy," he says.

"What? Who? Where are you?" I'm confused and frantic. What is going on?

"We are at the restaurant. Andy passed out. The ambulance is here and they are checking him."

God, I am struggling to handle all that is being laid on my path. Please, please, please let Andy be okay. I just need my boys to be okay.

He continues, "They want him to see a doctor."

"I'll meet you there."

Tommy and I race to get our shoes on, the dog harnessed, jackets on. I make sure we are all buckled in and head across town. The drive is a blur. A blur of traffic, red lights that take too long to change, a blur of songs on the radio, a blur of raindrops on the windows, a blur of thoughts and prayers and fears.

"Mommy, is Andy okay? What happened to him?" Tommy asks from the backseat with the puppy on his lap.

"I don't know what happened, honey. We are going to see him and try to find out."

"Is he fine?" Tommy furrows his brow, concerned. I don't know. I don't know the answer to this question, don't know a lot of things. There is so much that goes unexplained, especially in the moment. Sometimes the meaning of things are revealed later, and sometimes not. Lately I feel that there are too many of these occurrences in my life over a close span of time. I can't handle my kids being in danger, being threatened by fire, fever, unconsciousness. I can't handle even one more thing. This is past my optimum, beyond my capacity to deal.

"Let's pray for him," I respond, because really that is all we can do. Tommy nods, lowers his head, closes his eyes tightly. His little mouth moves with silent words, silent pleas for his big brother, his hero. My hero too. They both are my heroes. We drive, all the questions and worries and inconceivables forming a knot in my stomach and a lump in my throat.

Finally we arrive and I abruptly maneuver us into a parking space. It's dumping rain now. "Leave the dog," I instruct Tommy. He nods, pulling up his hood, and we make a run for it. We aren't concerned about the rain, we just want to see Andy.

And then there he is, sitting in the waiting room, white as a sheet. His eyes are not right. Glossy, dazed, wrong. I immediately put my hands on him. "Andy, how are you feeling right now?" He looks at me, but looks away, not wanting to talk. He makes a sound, part question, part grunt. "Are you nauseated? Does your head hurt? Do you feel lightheaded or pain anywhere?"

"No." Well at least he is speaking. The left side of his face is slightly swollen. That's strange, why only the one half? I am certain that I do not want to Google it at this point. One sure way to panic over symptoms is to search the internet for potential diagnoses. It can wait until after the doctor takes a look. I sit by him, his head on my shoulder and arm on my lap. My sweet boy, my first baby, my hero and love. All I can do is try not to hyperventilate and pray. I pray and pray and pray.

"Andy?" The nurse says in an open doorway. I stand, frantically motioning to his father to help hold and balance him as we all walk into the hallway, following the clipboard. Passing out, briefly at least, doesn't necessarily pose any health threats, but falling does. If he goes down we will catch him. We all shimmy into a room as the nurse takes his vitals and asks all the preliminary screening questions. I answer them like a Jeopardy contestant, as quickly and clearly as I can. No history of fainting. No heart problems. No health issues. No surgeries. No broken bones. No conditions, diseases, illness, fever. A perfectly healthy young boy. Who just randomly lost consciousness. What. The. Hell.

Then the story of the incident is retold by the Ken, because the doctor and I both need to hear it. They arrive at the restaurant, order food, wait. Andy gets pancakes, bacon, orange juice. They begin to eat, and make it part of the way through the meal. Andy has eaten maybe half of his food when he leans back and begins to take deep breaths. I immediately know that this is the yoga breathing we do. Both boys know to take calming breaths, in through the nose and out through the mouth. Slow and easy.

Ken continues with the story. Andy stops eating, and doesn't want anything more. This is unusual because he typically eats an inordinate amount of food right now. His face is pale, clammy, breaking a light sweat. At this point I would have had him lay down, legs bent, hoping it would pass. I've seen the signs in people about to pass out and they need to be down in a safe position. But no, it is decided to get up and walk out. I try to listen objectively to the rest of it with a neutral expression on my face.

"So I tell him, okay, if you aren't feeling well we can just go. You want to go? Let's go." his dad recaps. They slide out of the booth, stand up, and walk toward the door. Ken gets to the door, opens it up, and realizes Andy isn't behind him. He scans the restaurant, sees Andy over in the server area, clinging to a woman's arm and swaying. He runs over just in time to catch Andy as his eyes roll up and he passes out. The employees call 9-1-1, and here we are.

I look over Andy, making him raise up his shirt. No rash, no hives, no swelling of anything besides half of his face. No itching, no pain. I check all that I can think to check, and re-ask all the questions. What were you talking about? What is the last thing you remember? Did you feel sick to your stomach? How do you feel now? And then there is nothing left to check, nothing left to try to glean out of him. No possible explanations or hint to solve the mystery. Only worry and waiting remain.

We wait eternal, or at least it feels that way. There should be extra doctors on call just for kids who come in with mothers freaking out over their safety. Seriously, there should be zero waiting time with children. The light knock in the doorway lets me sigh, relieved. The doctor is here.

She steps in, all business and efficiency, which I love. This woman is not messing around. She looks at his eyes, in his mouth, nose, ears. She listens to his breathing, and then does a strength and balance evaluation that I have memorized from all of my visits to U.C. Davis Neurology. Do they think it was a stroke? His speech was fine, but his eyes still look wrong and he is clearly not himself. Pale, not wanting to speak, looking exhausted. This is not the normal energy level of my kid.

"Half of his face is slightly swollen," she observes, comparing sides.

"Yes, what does that mean?" I ask, afraid of the possible answers.

"I'm not certain, so we will do a full panel to check on him," she replies. Good, check it all. Take no chances. I glance at Andy. He's not going to like this.

We spend the next hour making sure he is stable and getting his fingers pricked for blood work. They don't get enough so he ends up with multiple tiny snips on his fingers and thumbs. "How will I use my tablet?" he asks, holding up his bandaged hands. The first normal thing he has said all morning. *Thank you, God.* If he is concerned about tapping with his thumbs he is thinking somewhat rationally. His energy begins to pick up, and finally my kid is back. I'm both relieved and still fearful. A lot of unanswered questions remain.

We wait on the tests, and finally we have an answer. "Anemic," the doctor says. I'm shocked. He is always so energetic, healthy, great diet. We go over all of this, and it just doesn't make sense. I share with her the recent health discovery of my very low B12 levels, which can cause a myriad of neurological issues and a specific type of anemia. I have to get monthly injections of B12 because regardless of my diet, because my body doesn't bind it properly. Maybe Andy has the same thing? The doctor agrees that it should definitely get checked out, and adds it to the list of tests he will be getting tomorrow morning at the lab.

She explains that his current level of something is at a 6, and that at level 4 they conduct blood transfusions. My ears seem to go temporarily deaf from the pressure of the blood flow through them. Um, what? This can't be right. The hypothetical scenario of that flashes through my mind until I forcefully shut it down. One moment at a time. Just be here in this moment. We are catching it and can correct it. Deep breath.

I schedule him a lab appointment for the early morning, though he doesn't need to fast. I just want the results being processed as soon as possible. We sign in, and Andy is subdued at the thought of having blood drawn. He's had it done but was much younger and has no recollection of it. We talk it out, and make a plan for him to look away as a precautionary measure. The lab assistant is very kind and walks him through all of the directions for a urine test and what the blood tests will be like. He walks down the hallway, glancing back at me, little cup in hand, and all I can do is again pray through this. *Just let him be okay.*

He returns to the tiny lab room and sits at the padded chair with an arm rest and they swab and band him and give him a poke. He closes his eyes and does his breathing. They take vial after vial after vial. I breathe. I watch him. I pray some more. He doesn't pale, doesn't shake, though it is clear he isn't a fan. But he's doing it. I talk to him a bit, try to distract him at least a little, and we get through it. And then the nurse is done, bandaging him up and chatting with him about baseball and watching him closely without showing it. She asks him to just sit and wait for a couple of minutes while she finishes up at the computer and then gives us the okay to go. Results should be available this week. More waiting, more praying. That's what this week's schedule looks like.

The next few days are stressful because we have no idea if or when he could just pass out again. I prepare him by explaining that he will be on constant supervision and I am the bailiff. He eats, I watch. He walks up the stairs, I escort. He showers, I give him three minute increments and check on him. He sits out of P.E. at school. Teachers and staff are alerted that it will take three months for his condition to stabilize after iron supplements, unless it turns out to be a B12 related intrinsic factor. Everyone is on stand by and monitoring him for falling or getting lightheaded. I pack granola bars and give him strict instructions to eat one on his break between classes. I buy him spinach, cook in an iron skillet, and feed him steak.

The week crawls by and it's Thursday and still no word on the results. I have to get out of the house. I also have to get more groceries, so I head to the grocery store nearby. I am looking blankly at the organic veggies when my phone rings. It's after hours so not the doctor, but I pick up anyway and identify myself.

"Hello, is this Andy's mom?" the female voice asks.

"Yes, it is."

"We have the results in for his lab work." I am both glad to hear it and uneasy at the same time.

"Okay, what did you find out?"

"Well, we need you to come back in to go over the results."

"What?" I ask, even though I hear her. I stand staring at the asparagus but not really seeing it. I just don't understand why this could be; all throughout my illness all of my test results were available to me online or over the phone. Even when the results weren't good, I still had remote access. She repeats herself, a little more slowly, "You need to come back in to go over the results."

I begin to panic, which causes my voice to raise an octave and come out too fast, "Is someone available to discuss them with me now, over the phone?"

"No, ma'am, I'm sorry, this needs to be gone over in the office. I have an opening tomorrow morning at eight a.m."

The panic turns to dark, ugly fear. What could it be? Leukemia? Some freak disease that causes kids to pass out?

And they suddenly have this magical appointment for first thing the very next day? How can this turn out to be anything short of horrific?

"I will be there tomorrow at eight." I thank her out of habit but my mind is reeling and the end of the call is a blur. My heart has dropped into my stomach. I roll the cart through the checkout line with whatever is already in there. It will have to be enough. I robotically unload the cart, hand over my bags, and manage to say something coherent to the cashier asking me how my day is going. I drive back to the house, grab my two bags of groceries, and try to keep it together.

I ask around about lab work results having to be read in person. Maybe this is a brand new thing that I've missed somehow. I chat with a couple of relatives, message friends, even bring it up to a colleague. We are all in agreement, all of us sharing the same understanding. Good news is typically revealed via a nurse over the phone. Requiring an in person visit to go over results is usually indicative of a medical condition of serious nature. I have an amazing group of people in all areas of my life. At work, in my family, the best friends anyone could want. They all pray for Andy, for us.

At dinner, I keep glancing over at Andy, wishing this to be better. I try to practice gratitude, because I know that some people can't have children, and some parents lose children in accidents, and that children can survive cancers and diseases and conditions. I know all of these things, and know that someone would willingly trade for the health that Andy does have, regardless of what the test results will reveal to us in the morning. And I am so grateful, grateful to know him and to love him and to have time with him. But that doesn't make this okay with me, and I pray harder than I thought I could right now. I'm exhausted, but somehow I muster up the strength to send that prayer full force, special delivery, urgent, handle with care. I don't just say the prayer, I feel the prayer, and the prayer is part of me, part of my heart and my mind and my very soul.

We go to bed but I don't sleep. I listen for Andy, and wrap my arms around him when he cuddles up to me. I breathe in the smell of his hair, feel his warm feet against mine, and gently stroke his forehead. I sit propped up in the bed, the feel of his breathing steady and even against my side, and I close my eyes and listen to the rhythm of it all night long. Eventually, the sun breaks through the layer of clouds and falls into the room. I am still awake as the streams of light grow brighter and I can now begin counting down the hours until we know.

Chapter 24

But the Lord stood with me, and strengthened me.

2 Timothy 4:17

The not knowing is a blessing and a curse. A blessing in that the ignorance of what it might be is still protective in a way, and there is the hope that it could all just be a bad mistake, like a bad dream that settles into your morning like the chill of winter sneaking in through the door jambs. The curse of it is that until we know, we can't begin to deal with it. The unknown prohibits a plan of action or identification of coping mechanisms. This is exactly why fear and anxiety are such burdens to bear. If it is the fear of the unknown, there is nothing you can do with that. I often hear that worry is like a rocking chair. You are moving, expending energy, but getting nowhere. My rocker is going a mile a minute over this. The wait is excruciating, because I can't make a plan. There are just a thousand possibilities, a thousand what ifs, occupying my mind space. As we sit in the waiting room I am grateful that this is about to change, and it's mixed with dread at hearing the diagnosis.

Andy is called in, and we go through the motions of weighing, measuring, taking the temperature. We enter the small room and he hops up on the exam table, rustling the hygienic paper beneath him. We wait the longest twelve minutes in the history of waiting until a quick rap on the door makes me jump.

"Thank you for coming in today," the doctor says, quickly spanning the room and pulling up information on the computer.

"Of course. What did the tests show?" I ask, unable to make polite small talk.

"So, the thing is, they all came back completely normal," she explains, looking baffled.

"Normal? There's nothing wrong?" I don't even dare to hope this is correct until I've heard it again.

"Completely normal." She nods, looking at the monitor as she scrolls over the numerous tests.

"B12 is fine?" I want to make sure on this one.

"Yes, all fine."

"And the anemia?"

"That's the thing, his levels are all perfect."

"So, he's not anemic at all?"

"Not even a little." She offers a small smile as she continues to review whatever is on the list.

"So, the first test determining his level was wrong?"

"Yes, and it's very common to have false positives with that particular test. We are actually getting new tests in with the hopes that the error margin will be less."

"I see," I say slowly. It crosses my mind to consider being irritated, because this information would have been useful. Not to mention that these results could have and should have been released over the phone, saving me a sleepless, fretful night. The doctor's voice pulls me back to the here and now, in this small, sterile space.

"For now, we are going to assume that the passing out was an isolated occurrence, possibly an allergic reaction. Let me know immediately if it occurs again. If it doesn't, plan to bring him back in three months and we will do more lab work to retest everything to confirm results."

Any irritation I am feeling dissipates because I'm too damn relieved to complain. There is only room in my heart for the gratefulness I feel and for the love I have for this kid. He is okay. He is a perfectly healthy kid. *Thank you God. Thank you so much. Thank you thank you thank you.* My prayers were heard. My prayers were answered. Andy is fine.

The test results don't stop me from conducting further research online regarding pre-teens and loss of consciousness. It turns out that puberty can cause a vast array of issues in the bodies and minds of pre-pubescent and pubescent children. We hear about the temper flares, the insatiable appetites, the struggle for independence, the constant challenging of boundaries, the wild range of emotions. We hear stories about our sweethearts transforming into little beasts that begin to stink and defy and push. But I haven't heard about puberty resulting in a child passing out. Apparently it isn't uncommon at all, and many factors can contribute such as not being hydrated enough, hormone fluctuations, and growth spurts. It doesn't explain Andy's slight swelling on one side of his face, but everything else makes sense to support that this last growth spurt and changing voice are likely the culprit of his incident.

In the coming months, I work on communicating to him and to Tommy explanations about what is occurring physically, and how that also impacts emotional reactions. I make a point of touching base with them each week about how we can better support each other through all we are experiencing. I begin working with Andy one on one, too, and openly share my perspective about decisions, boundaries, privileges, and responsibilities. I give him more responsibilities and assign tasks that are appropriate for his age, and I always explain to him that I do not like to take away privileges but that it is a necessary part of good parenting to instill life lessons.

We have several discussions on the comment made at drop off, and he struggles to understand why I am not like one of his friends at school, all of whom roast each other for fun. It has taken a few months, but finally he is mellowing out and learning that our relationship is unique to us. He is learning that as we redefine our relationship with the changes he is encountering, that the roles for now remain the same. I am a mother first, friend second.

As his trauma symptoms are lessening we are growing close again and I see marked changes in his disposition and ability to cope appropriately. He is still a pre-teen, but we are getting to the point of being able to face this under more normal circumstances as opposed to hormones plus PTSD, which is an awful combination. The more the trauma symptoms wear off, the more I see my kid return to his old self, laughing and playing with his little brother, doing helpful things for all of us, and giving my heart relief that he is recovering and that I get to see the progress every day.

I get to see him cuddle with Tommy again as they watch funny videos, play with the puppy and kiss her every night, and feel him snuggle against my arm in the wee hours of the night when we both can't sleep. I get to see him show up for baseball practice every day, and support his little brother with encouraging comments and advice when Tommy makes the All Star team and Andy doesn't. I get to see him morph both back into the boy that he once was and the man that he will one day become, a twelve year old man-child full of doing the right thing, helping others, and always speaking the truth.

Mysterious things happen all of the time, and in the case of mysterious health issues, all we can do is pray and seek out the best medical attention that is available. I prayed, we all prayed, for Andy to be well, to be healed, and to have this issue go away and not come back. There are no words to describe how hard I prayed. I continue to pray for my boys throughout each day, and they pray too. I think that for as many mysteries are out there, there are a multitude more of miracles. I am living proof, Andy is living proof, all around us is living proof. As for his loss of consciousness and strange swelling of the face, it never happens again.

Chapter 25

He will never leave you nor forsake you. Do not be afraid; do not be discouraged.

Deuteronomy 31:8

We are finally all well, over the barrage of respiratory illnesses that plagued our winter season. The warmer days bring with them less viruses and infections. My physical recovery from long term illness and nerve damage continues to progress and I have many more good days than bad. Yet I wait for several months before considering making the drive back up to our property and the remains of what was once our home. I tell myself I am not ready, the boys are not ready. I tell myself the weather is too bad. I tell myself I have other things to do. I tell myself it can wait. And all of it is true.

I avoid insurance meetings on the property, and instead provide footage and photographs from the press to claims adjusters. The photos are grim and unreal. Like everything has just been blasted off of the foundation. Like everything has been edited out. Like it has all just disappeared. And it has. The mere thought of being back on that road, our path of deliverance, increases my heart rate. I wonder if the drive can induce an anxiety attack. I don't experience them, but for some reason I think I might when faced with the memories of narrowly escaping from that burning mountain, navigating on that winding, flame engulfed road through the devastation, through the small remnants of a town that once was.

I hear every day the stories of people going back up, sifting for treasures, hoping to find that piece of jewelry, that heirloom ring of Grandma's, a vase of someone's ashes, a wedding band. Some people are lucky in the search efforts. Some are not. Every person I speak to or read about on social media goes up with the intention of getting closure and yet they mostly report that they come back feeling worse. No one is prepared for the level of mass destruction they see all around them. Trees are gone. Businesses are gone. Homes are gone. You can see for miles because nothing blocks the view. It is all blackened, ashen, dead.

Warped skeletons of cars remain, the windshields hanging in pools of dripping glass from the dashboards, steering columns, and window frames. Chimney tombstones stand lonely amidst the now desolate terrain. Metal staircases that lead to nothing rise up from the rubble. It's difficult to even find addresses because there are no markers, no indicators of what used to be. People go up and experience not only their own grief, but the losses of others as well. Even strangers, people from the press, report that it is depressing, tragic, gruesome. You can't go up and not be affected by the visual assault that grips your heart, tightens your stomach, waters the eyes with tears. The images are not easily erased from the mind, which instead plays them back in slow motion like an old black and white film.

And in fact it is all black and white; there is no color at all. The trees are black, and the once orange soil is now ashen and gray. Cars are all just melted metal, charred and dark, no specks left at all of the once blues, reds, greens. No colorful signs or garden art sculptures catch the eye, gracing front yards. There are no yards. The photography is depressing and the palate deathly. It looks like a wasteland that will take many more years to rebuild than people are estimating.

I stay down in Chico, we all stay in Chico, refusing to drive through the terror zone again. I wait and wait some more, until I feel that it won't undo the healing I've worked so hard to attain. Until I feel that Andy is ready. Until we are strong enough to see it, face it, feel it. It takes over four months to get to this point. We are all sitting at the table having breakfast when the topic arises.

"Mom, I want to go up. I want to go see it for myself," Andy says, confident in his decision.

"Not me. I don't want to go. Do I have to go?" Tommy asks, confident in his decision too, but unsure about how the situation will go down.

"No, Tommy, you don't have to go up. I don't think you should." They both look at me, waiting for my response to Andy. I nod my head slowly, rubbing my temples and thinking about it yet again. I have already put hours of thought into this decision making process. He has mentioned repeatedly that he wants to go back up to see it. I listen to both sides of my brain; he is still young and doesn't need to be traumatized again, he is becoming a young man and acted as such, the visions of destruction are difficult to let go, seeing it might facilitate closure, seeing it might trigger PTSD symptoms, yes, no, maybe, I don't know. I breathe out a long, slow breath that I don't know I am holding until I release it back into the wild. I stare at Andy, my little man-child. He is just entering puberty and the physical changes over the last few months are striking. Looking at him, I know that I don't want to choose for him. He deserves to choose, deserves to have some say in his own healing. I can't determine that for him. He acted in a brave, calm, compassionate manner throughout our ordeal, and earned the right to decide on his own.

I tell him all of this, and he nods, understanding.

"But I do have to make you aware of what people have said after going up there. It's very saddening, and not everyone is gaining the closure they seek. Most everyone says that it makes it worse. They also are not finding items during the sifting process in our area. The fire was just too hot. If we go up, we will have to wear protective gear because of the toxins. It's going to be emotional."

He agrees and still feels prepared. Or maybe he is just young and strong and resilient.

"I want it to be just us. Just you and me," he says.

"Me too, Andy. We will do it together." I squeeze his hand, still having doubts about the whole thing but ultimately knowing he needs to do this. He needs to see that there is nothing left, needs to be able to walk the property in order to leave it behind. We will make the drive back up soon when the torrential rains let up and the risk of flooding and rock slides lifts.

Spring break hits and we need it like never before. The Christmas holiday was not restorative, not relaxing, not regenerative. We all need to just eat junk food, laze around in our pj's, sleep in, and watch movies. We need to do this several times. I plan for it, getting groceries for easy meals, chips and salsa, snacks and chocolate. I even get soda pop. We need to chill out. We have our first meal of the break, tacos. They taste amazing, especially now that I have an appetite back post illness. I am grateful every time I take a bite of food that isn't forced down just to stay alive.

The tacos stand no chance against me and two growing boys who now have baseball practice and workouts. We eat them all and Tommy still wants more. I excuse Andy to go shower and Tommy and I sit at the table while he finishes eating. I share with him the plan for the next day.

"Hey, you're going with your dad tomorrow so Andy and I can drive up to the property, okay?" I say conversationally. We've been planning it for a couple of weeks now.

"What? Tomorrow? No. Mommy. Mommy, don't go." His voice is panicked, eyes filling with tears. I get up from my chair and hug him while he sits perched on the edge of his seat. "Tommy, it's okay," I try to reassure him.

"Can you call me on the drive?" His voice is frantic and small and heartbreaking.

"I don't think there is cell service yet. Maybe, but I can't promise to call you until we get back because I don't know if I can or not."

"I don't want you guys to go." His neck and face are getting flushed, red and splotchy. He seems allergic to the thought of us driving up there. "Mommy, I'm panicking," he says.

"Okay, look at me, breathe with me." I take his little hands in mind and gently squeeze. "In for a count of three, hold for a count of three, out slowly for a count of three. In through the nose, two, three, hold, two three, out through the mouth, two, three. Repeat." We do this several times until he can focus.

"Now you breathe and I will talk," I say. He nods, breathing in through his sweet little nose. I quietly and calmly talk him through the situation. "There is no possibility of fire. One, there is nothing left to burn, and two, it is all wet now and not fire season. I would not go up if there were any safety concerns, do you know that?" I ask him. He nods again. "Good. Mommy will not take any chances with safety, okay?"

"I'm just scared."

"I understand, but really, this will be okay."

I have to remember that he was traumatized that day too. I put myself in his perspective the day of the fire. He sees the monstrous smoke plume from the schoolyard, sees someone else's car arrive to pick him up, sees that everyone is freaking out that I haven't called. He sees it get dark that night and still no one has heard from me. It has been over six hours since Mommy, big brother, and puppy had run on foot from the deadliest force of nature our part of the world has seen. He sees that it isn't right, sees that we might not have made it out. And the thought of us willingly returning and driving through it again seems unfathomable to him. Parts of me agree.

Parts of me don't ever want to return to the scene of the crime. I am tempted to let time and new memories push it all back to the cold storage section of my memory and leave it frozen there, buried underneath an icy layer of pain and fear. Parts of me want to ignore it and focus on the future, on the here and now, on all that is positive and sunshine and unicorns. Only I know this strategy doesn't work. The dark memories find a way to seep out, the fears floating to the surface when least expected. They don't stay buried, they don't stay frozen. They will wait to haunt me if I don't face them and allow them release. I must face the road with all its scars, the terrain with all its burns, and the ashen remains of the house if I am to heal and discover peace. My desire for peace is greater than my fear. We will leave in the morning.

Chapter 26

The Lord is close to the brokenhearted; He rescues those whose spirits are crushed.

Psalm 34:18

The next morning after Tommy is gone Andy and I load up the car. We pack waters, snacks, the dog, hoodies, hand trowels, gloves, masks, a large wooden and screen sifter box. It feels like a reenactment of the evacuation packing but more solemn. We are both quiet as we fit everything into the back. I can't get in the car now without thinking about how we might have to potentially escape something. Is there enough gas? Do we have blankets? What shoes are we all wearing? What if we have to hike on foot somewhere for some freak reason? What if? It's not rational, it's not logical, but it is there. Andy asks to hold the dog on his lap and I know the what ifs are there for him, too. I tell him sure, she'd like that, and I try not to make a big deal out of something that really is a big deal. In fact it's huge, of epic, life changing proportions.

We get in the car, the same dependable Toyota that drove us out of Hell itself, and begin the drive across town to Skyway, the main road up to Paradise. The first bit of the trip is normal except for the fact that we know we are returning to the battlefield of the war between Good and Evil. Out of the car windows, the world around us is continuing. The season shifts just as if nothing happened at all on the eighth of November. The birds are out, the sun is shining, and the air smells of the honey sweet almond blossoms that are in full glory in the next town over.

When I was a young child living out in the orchards I called them popcorn trees. They do look as if they are covered in popcorn at a glance. Big, white puffs cling in dense bunches, contrasting starkly against the nearly black bark. Upon closer inspection the petals are a translucent blush color, with deeper pink centers and a heavenly scent. Breathing them in takes me back to simpler times, lighter days. It gives me a temporary, welcomed distraction from our current mission. I keep the windows open to allow the perfumed air to flow all around us.

As we turn onto Skyway and make our way up the hill, the smell wafting in isn't honey sweet anymore. It smells dank and burnt, like a wet bag of charred food. It is soon clear that the fire was just as destructive as we remember, worse even than we knew, because now it is daylight and we are seeing all of it for miles. There are places where the new grasses can't even grow and the ground is still blackened. Once monstrous pine trees are now reduced to lonely charred spikes sticking up like war spears, ugly and final. Our tribe was obliterated. We don't speak.

Some burned areas have been partially washed away, making the terrain look raw and exposed. Ironically right after the fire this area experienced torrential rainfall, creating mudslides and flooding. Naturally sloped hills are compromised by fire and are weakened causing debris to be mobile and a risk when subjected to heavy rains. We see that the embankments now have more clearance and new rocks and boulders reveal their stony faces through the mud. I wouldn't want to be on some of these mountain roads during a storm right now. It's stressful enough on a clear and sunny day.

We start to see remnants of buildings, charred pieces of would be structures scattered on the landscape. We see crews of workers taking down trees. The *Town of Paradise* sign was destroyed, and the wooden word *Paradise* now rests low to the ground. That will probably be one of the first things that gets replaced. I slow the car as we move up the hill and near the edge of the town.

"Oh no. Wow."

"What are those?"

"They represent each person who didn't make it out."

"Oh." The weight of his word hangs heavy and slow in the air, blocking any other responses. There are no words, only the clenching of the gut and the squeezing of the heart. These are the members of our community, of our churches and stores and schools.

To the left of us are eighty five crosses, white and side by side, one for each life lost in the fire. They are bright and tall and heartbreaking, hammered into the recovering soil. The line stretches far up the hillside and curves around into the distance. There are so many for what was such a small town. Wives, sons, grandparents, friends, uncles, fathers, mothers, cousins, children, dads, husbands, sisters, brothers.

I pull over and get out, slowly walking the length of the line of crosses. A name is on each one, making it more personal, more real, more heart wrenching than just the numbers. My stomach tightens, my chest constricts, my whole being is squeezed with pain for people who didn't make it out, for their families left behind to crawl through the grief. My eyes blur before I can read each name. Joyce, Rafaela, Carol, Julian, David, Larry, Andrew, Joanne, Barbara, Dennis, John, Gordon, Andrew, Robert, Rose, Jean, Elizabeth, Sally, James, Richard, Dennis, Jennifer, Christina, Lou, Evva, TK, Gary, Dorothy, Sara, John, Joanne, David, Deborah, Helen, Joy, Beverly, Forrest, Vernice, Frederick, Sheila, John, Don, Larry, Russel, Victoria, Shirlee, Ellen, Donna, David, Ernest, Jesus, Carl, Paula, Randall, Teresa, Richard, Marie, Kimber, Joseph, Joan, Vincent, Warren, Kathy, Anna, James, Cheryl, Robert, Berniece, Chris, Ronald.

Some of the crosses remain blank because not everyone has been identified yet.

The sadness is overwhelming, and I take a moment to let it course through my being. And then it hits me, like a blow to the chest. Our names aren't listed on the top of a cross here. My children, my mother, grams, aunts, uncle, cousin, me. We are not represented here; we all made it out. Thank you God for that, for everything. At the base of the crosses, some have flowers, one has a necklace, some have notes, one has an image of the Virgin Mary. I don't bother to stop the tears as I pray for the loved ones that are grieving, for those who lost the most.

Of all the lives lost, none were children. I find this both miraculous and difficult to comprehend. How many thousands of children were evacuated from all of the schools that day? How many children rode down the hill with strangers that saved them? I know of parents that stayed behind to help others, who sent their kids on before them, and of parents who couldn't get to their children at various schools. I know for damn certain that if someone, anyone, could have safely gotten Andy out I would have sent him on without me.

Of all the crosses here, not a single one represents that of a child. The youngest person lost was thirty nine years old. And while every life is painful to lose, and every life worth saving, the lost life of a child is the hardest to grieve. Especially a young child who hasn't really yet lived his or her life. I would not be surprised if every single person on one of these crosses would have willingly traded his or her own life to save that of a child. Every child made it out. Every. Single. Child. How does that happen in a disaster of these proportions? Every single kid in high school, all of the middle schoolers, every single student at all of the elementary and preschools escaped that day. An estimated five thousand students were evacuated. Five thousand. That doesn't include any youngsters not yet in school. That is an enormous number of children. All accounted for.

Here in this moment, I am sad, but I am also grateful. Grateful that Andy is in the group of children who all survived despite the odds, despite the enormity of destruction. In a deadly fire that seemingly had no mercy, somehow every single child was spared. I am grateful for every child that is meant to be here, meant to have this experience of survival and to later do something with it to better the world in his or her own way. I pray for their healing, continued protection, and for one day gaining an understanding of their paths. I slowly head back to the car, still in prayer, still in awe, still in grief.

We keep driving uphill and slowly enter the town that once was. We stop at the first intersection, turn right, and wait to enter the parking lot leading to a church that is distributing clean up kits. Traffic delays are expected because so much tree work is happening all around. Once we are allowed to pass, we sign in at the church and collect Hazmat suits, booties to cover shoes, buckets with cleaning supplies, extra gloves, and masks. I gather what we need and haul it all back out to the car. It doesn't take long before we begin to wonder where we are. Some business signs are legible, but many are gone or so warped they are indecipherable. Almost all of the buildings are unrecognizable if they are even standing. Most of them are leveled. The few structures left standing are primarily cement blocks, the barren rectangles of previous windows and doorways empty of any wood or glass. Like dead eyes they stare back at us, blank and unyielding. Warped metal roofing pieces and hollow shells of cars and trucks remain.

The views of what was downtown is now miles of charred parts of trees, and deep canyons that were once blocked from sight by lush green forestry. New power lines are in place in some areas, the fresh wooden poles a stark contrast to the burns everywhere else. They are the only new things visible so far. We try to locate our former hangouts, asking each other if that pile of rubble was such and such. For the most part we just aren't sure.

The twenty minutes up feels both longer and shorter. I'm glad we are doing it, just the three of us again, facing our fears. Andy breaks the silence. "Oh, Harley is shaking. Put your hand back here to soothe her." Andy coos at her, holding her tightly on his lap. Maybe she smells that everything is burned? Does she remember where we are? She is only a year old now, but dogs are amazing. She senses something. I look in the rearview mirror and she is definitely shaking all over. That's really strange. I reach back and talk to her, letting her lick my hand, reassuring all of us that there is no threat. No danger. No risk. No fire. Andy and I make eye contact in the rearview mirror. "We got this, kid. You and me."

"Yep," is all he says as we continue our way up, working backward from that fateful day. We reach the stoplight at the intersection of Skyway and Clark. The intersection where it all went down. I breathe. Tony's smog shop is gone. The gas station is still intact. Wow. We both look to the left as we roll slowly through the light, finding our little cement slab of survival. It is all blocked off with cones and caution tape to deter traffic, not that it would stop me, but I just don't feel like walking that ground today, and neither does Andy. Another time perhaps. We stay en route and continue up the hill.

"Hey, that's where we stopped to pee," Andy observes. I look, and yes it is, though barely recognizable. "And that's where the Pepsi truck was parked," I point out, noticing that there are still red brake lights adhered to the pavement in that spot. No way would we have gotten out alive from that metal box. We slowly round the mountain curves, Sawmill Peak jutting up into the skyline without anything blocking the view. The Depot, an old train station turned restaurant, is gone. They had just reopened after renovating from a kitchen fire. Damn. I feel for everyone. Every business owner, every employee, every homeowner, renter, resident. Thousands of different situations, and my heart aches for each and every one.

We exit Paradise and enter Magalia, crossing over the bridge. These once familiar views are foreign now. Gone is the feeling that I know this road like the back of my hand. Gone is the feeling that I am driving home. Gone is all that is familiar. I can't tell what is now from what used to be. What was a tree lined drive is now a bare, steep, canyon route. It looks nothing like our typical commute back to the house, which is probably a blessing. I'm not homesick on this drive, I'm disoriented. We push through and I head toward the little grocery store that is now open again. Just to see something in color, some form of life up here, some type of recovery. I grab us some food from the hot bar and wait in the long line with exhausted Cal Fire crews, soot and dirt covered PG&E workers, and residents that still look shell shocked. People make eye contact and nod, but we are all quiet, tired, weary. Typically in this situation in California, someone would start the complaining rants about the slow, long, line with only one checkout open, and others would chime in agreeing and disgruntled. But this isn't a typical situation; not even close to the norm. Instead we all just silently wait, either grateful for the store surviving and reopening or too tired to bitch about the long line, or a combination of both. The person in front of me tries his credit card five times. Finally it goes through. There is nothing rushing our attempt at some emotional closure up here today. I eventually get back to the car and hand Andy his container of food. He devours both his and mine in the parking lot like a twelve year old hyena. I give him some time to digest before we go to the property. Just in case.

I wind through the little streets, stopping at one intersection and looking around to figure out if I'm going the right way. "I think it's to the left," Andy says, and I agree. But I have to count the stops to be sure. We pass a school that is intact, or at least the cafeteria is.

"We could have survived there and had cafeteria food," Andy observes.

"Yeah and a bathroom," I reply. That would have been appreciated. Never take for granted clean drinking water and a functional toilet. Toilet paper is also a bonus in life.

Finally, we arrive at our street and it makes no sense to see the random, two wooden houses that stand alone. Nothing is different to set them apart from every other structure that didn't survive. There are trees around them, and burned lots, and they host gutters full of leaves and pine needles. One is directly across the street from our property and used to belong to my dear neighbor Sadie. She is in Oregon now, the view out of her kitchen window here too desolate to take. That window perfectly frames the remains of our place. The view that was once a lush garden of herbs and grasses, two little boys playing with the puppy or riding their mini ATVs, the little house on the hill that hosted dinners and birthdays and sun tea on the porch. She couldn't stay and look at what once was all around her. She listed her house and it sold in three days for a ransom. I look around for any signs of the new neighbors, but there are none.

We slow and drive by the property. The driveway is covered in debris, rubble, pools of hardened metal blobs. I park across the street and for a minute we just sit there and stare. There is nothing to say, no words of consolation, no humor to lighten the situation. No way around it. I finally break the trance and pop the back open, leaving the windows all down for the dog. I don't want her walking in this, sniffing ash and whatever else is in the ruins. We suit up, hazmat ready, and walk across the street in our bootie covered shoes and toward the driveway.

Long scratch marks curve down the cement drive. It takes me a minute to register that they are from the corpse of our Honda being drug down it. I guess that makes sense that they just drag the cars because there are no wheels. A tow truck couldn't make it up the driveway right now. Melted pools of what is likely aluminum glint in the sunlight in abstract globules. The biggest pine I have ever seen is gone, a leveled stump all that remains. It looks like a giant, low, lonely table. We both turn in slow motion to face the house area. Gnarled patio furniture lies on a thin bed of ashes. The foundation outlines what used to be, looking like far less than nine hundred square feet. My mind flashes on a wooden sign that hung in the dining room, a gift from one of my friends at work. *Love grows best in tiny houses.* It sure did for us. I hand Andy a trowel and muffle out directions through my mask, "Here you go. Be careful where you step, rusty nails are everywhere."

    We crouch and dig, dragging rusty metal pieces of ductwork off the top layer of debris. We map out rooms the best we can and hope to find pieces of the past. Andy looks to find crystals he and Tommy collected, and I dig for a little ceramic pot Andy made for me in kindergarten. I rake and dig and remap the area, and dig some more. I know I am close because little pieces of the fine China set my dad sent his mother during the war are right here. I rearrange debris, shards of elegant Noritake all around. I break a sweat, and still find nothing. There is nothing.

    We dig for hours, and only find three crystals that were cracked and faded from the fire. Their light is gone. We should just rebury them, but Andy wants to return them to his brother. He also finds part of his coin collection, small rusted disks that are unidentifiable. He makes a tiny pile of the recovered items. It's major work for minimal to no reward. I realize that nothing survived this fire unscathed, including us. Anything that made it is now an altered version of the original state, still here but different now.

    I stop and survey the perimeter. Friends in other fire areas shared that many plants came back to life, sprouting up from deep roots. I was hopeful, but there is literally nothing sprouting up, nothing to dig and transplant elsewhere. It is all just gone, completely and utterly gone. My grandmother, a master gardener, has a phrase that is always with me when a plant dies. *Back to the earth.* I try to use this cyclical explanation to ease the losses. My photographs, the boys' artwork, my recipes, my bible, the Christmas angels. All recycled now, and back to the earth. No new grasses have begun again up here yet, but it will happen eventually. The land will recover.

I sigh and look further, past the house area and into the miles upon miles of mess. Everywhere I turn lies tons and tons of debris. This recovery and rebuilding process is going to take so much longer than everyone thinks. This isn't a two year plan here. This is more like five years to get through clean up phases and begin to put up structures, and even longer to reestablish as an entire community. Ten years maybe?

One example are the water lines. The meters were all covered with durable plastic lids, which warped and melted into the water system and released benzene, a highly toxic chemical. The few homes that are standing up here don't have a clean water source. And it's not just undrinkable. They recommend not using it at all. It's potentially more dangerous to shower in it than to ingest it because the evaporative process increases the amount of benzene released. Sadly, it is better in many ways to lose everything and get the insurance money to start over rather than have to live up here and have no water and none of your neighbors.

I try to take a deep breath, but even through the mask I can smell the pungent, carboniferous odor that wafts on the breeze. It smells like ground zero here. It smells like utter ruin and cauterized memories. One lone daffodil bobs it's sunny head amongst the ashes and rubble, but it isn't spring here. This isn't any season at all. I don't know what this is. I turn toward my son, the only peace or joy I can find here. My heart hurts as I watch him, crouching down, digging for something, anything, of what once was. Maybe he feels my eyes on him, or maybe he's just ready to let it all go, because he stands and faces me.

"Hey," I say, as I meet his gaze.

"Hey," he says back, resolutely. I slowly nod my understanding, because with our eyes we say so much more. We say how hard this is, how disappointing it is to want so badly to get back what made our house a home and not be able to find it, how incomprehensible it is to literally dig through feet of sooty ashes that are our things turned to dust, how tired and weary we are from not being home. Maybe I should cry, let out more of the grief and leave it here with the ruins of our previous life, but right now I'm just too damn tired and I can tell that my kid feels the same way.

"You done for today?" I ask him, breaking the knowing silence that hangs in the space between us.

"Yeah, I'm done."

"Me too, kiddo."

We meet on the outskirts of the rubble and walk side by side over the crunching charcoal and glass and ash, leaving our bucket of supplies on the huge tree stump table, not concerned that it might be gone when we return. There is no thieving to be had here and the miscreants know it. There is nothing to steal, nothing to find. Nothing to salvage. We peel off our sweaty gloves and bag them up with our hazmat gear and masks. At least now maybe Andy can get some peace, get to mentally leave it all behind. I desperately wish that for him, and I hold on to that thin glimmering filament of hope as I walk away from the fifteen years of love and nurturing and remodeling that were poured into our little nest. We silently head down the driveway together, load up into the car, pull out onto our former street, and don't look back.

Chapter 27

Have patience, God isn't finished yet.

Philippians 1:6

When I was hunting for my first house it was exciting, and full of new possibilities. The future was bright, I had a salary and benefits, I was young and healthy. I was upgrading from an apartment with paper thin walls, shopping for more privacy and some quiet. From my apartment, I could hear snoring and all the bathroom activities on one side, and the warm up rehearsals for choir practice on the other. Fa la la la la la la. Fa la la la la la la. Over and over, and over again. And with a terrible voice. He probably had parents that falsely convinced him he was talented enough to win on American Idol. I encourage my boys but I am honest and realistic too. They won't be rock stars. Neither will my previous neighbor.

I endured tour after tour of fixer uppers that were still likely to stretch my budget despite realtors calling them affordable. But I wasn't worried about the money at that time, as I did have a great job and no one else who needed me. No husband, no kids, no dog. My expenses were minimal so I could afford to take a chance on investing in a house. I saw washing machines in the kitchen, cheap and worn astroturf on patios, and hot pink ceiling to floor cabinets. None of it fazed me because I was energetic enough to strip old wood and repaint, to creatively make a tiny space work, and to put years and money into improvements, breathing new love into an old space.

Part of the joy of my first home was that it didn't have shared walls. It was spaced out on a third of an acre with neighbors but no fences, no other houses right on top of mine. We all had wide open space. And though the house was only nine hundred square feet, it was almost double the size of my apartment, plus there was a one car garage, a large deck, a small shed, and a loft space. The idea of buying instead of renting was appealing to me as well. I'd be putting money toward my own retirement, not a landlord's.

House hunting post fire is not an enjoyable experience like it was before. It isn't fun like shopping for shoes or plants or cars with the luxury of not having to replace items because of a disaster. In fact, it is depressing and surreal walking through other people's spaces, seeing their things, their photos, their decor. Our place was small, so we don't have a big cash out from the insurance. We might get just enough for a down payment and then I will have to mortgage the rest. Despite this challenge, I am hoping to afford a place that we can grow into a little. Before I know it I will have teenage boys and want separate bathrooms if I can manage it.

The first house we view that falls within my budget has no flooring or baseboards and needs to be gutted further. We walk through on creaky plywood, looking at the dark, tiny rooms. The kitchen and baths need serious demo. This is beyond fixer upper. We are talking Property Brothers take it down to the bare studs level of renovation needed. The house is less than twelve hundred square feet, with a huge yard and only slightly ghetto neighborhood. It needs so much work, and I don't know if I can financially or emotionally afford to renovate again this soon. I had just renovated our little place. We walk outside and take one last look around, thanking the realtor. I put it on the maybe list.

The second house is newer, brighter, and has a little more square footage. It is small, but very tastefully done. The yard is miniscule and that means no baseball, no garden, and really low maintenance. The owner, an investor, is asking for an obscene amount of money and will certainly get it. I find out through a realtor that the owner is renting to a local sheriff who offered a fair price to buy it and his offer was declined. He will be out in two weeks. In a city, no actually in a county with no rentals, no decent prices for homes. No apartments, no RV spaces, no rooms to rent. I say a prayer for him that he can find housing now that his lease will be terminated. All for what, for the seller to gain an extra thirty grand of profit? Fifty grand maybe? It won't be from me.

  The third house is perfect. It is in a great neighborhood by the schools and the little league parks, in a newer division that hopefully means I won't be renovating or doing major home repairs anytime soon. The interior colors are great; I won't even have to paint. We tour it, and the boys are right at home, checking it all out and clearly enjoying it. The kitchen table is even similar to the one we had. It will be a stretch financially, but with the loan I am prequalifying for and the extra hours of counseling, I can just manage it. My realtor and I talk about numbers and she suggests I write a letter about our family to submit with the offer. I send it to her and we agree on the amount, and she begins the process of putting in an official offer. I'm actually looking forward to this potentially being our new place, which is surprising. I didn't know I could feel this optimistic this soon. It's a good sign and I let it course through me, giving me hope and energy and motivation to keep moving forward.

  A couple of hours pass and I get an unexpected call from the mortgage lender. I pick up and know right away from his tone of voice that this isn't news I am going to want to hear. He clears his throat and struggles to get through the initial pleasantries before delivering the unfortunate message. My position at the University is temporary and has been on my work history list less than six months so they can't count that income. Okay, I think, it isn't a large amount anyway and it is only for half the academic year. We can just use the community college income, right? Wrong.

  Apparently in California when you apply for a mortgage, the work history has to be two years or longer. In my mind this is not an issue since I have been at the college for twenty five years. They can just verify my paychecks for proof of income. And besides, my credit history is stellar. I mention this to the lending rep.

He clears his throat again and I hear the whisper of a painful sigh. "Well, yes, but the thing is...the thing is that with your recent medical leave and now returning to work in a new capacity, your history doesn't show two years yet. And we can't go off of current pay stubs, we have to go off of taxes. You barely worked last year because of your illness recovery. So we can't make you the loan. I feel terrible about this. I just wish there was something I could do to help."

Well, hell. I did not see that coming. I paid my mortgage on time, every month, for fifteen years. Even on bed rest. Even through a year of being on sick leave. Even when my paychecks stopped. Every month was on time, in full. Purchasing without a mortgage loan means we get way less house. And I mean waaaay less. Oh wow. I finish up the call and sit in the car and breathe. Damn. I have to stop the offer on the house. Damn damn damn. I call my realtor with the news about the loan and mentally walk away from the house, refusing to think about how great it was for us. It sells the next day for cash.

The housing market continues to go insane. By insane I mean that the house across the street from where we are staying sells for one hundred thousand dollars over the already inflated asking price. People are writing checks for homes that cost over half a million dollars without needing to finance. The average amount being paid over the asking price for homes in my price range is approximately sixty thousand dollars. Bidding wars are unavoidable, and whoever has the most money, usually in cash, gets the house. I am not in a position to even compete. Apartment complexes have a six month waitlist. Most aren't even adding to the lists because they know they cannot possibly accommodate all of the need. Part of the problem was waiting so long to hear if the house had made it or not. Until I had verification, I couldn't file the insurance claims. Homes that were on the outskirts of the fire were easiest to document as gone, so those owners were the first in line for insurance funds and rental places to live. We continue to stay where we are and save every penny as we wait out the market. It can't last forever, it only feels like it does.

  We wait two months. We wait three months. Four, five, six. All of us crammed into a queen sized bed for which I am eternally grateful. Little league season helps to pass the time as we wait to be able to afford a place of our own. With two boys playing baseball the practice and game schedules are intense. Added to the schedule are my new counseling hours and other employment opportunities. I take on some trade work under the table for a baseball academy in town which allow the boys access to an indoor facility, coaching, and clinics. I teach and counsel at the college during the day, then work on grants, advertising, and the academy website at night and on weekends. *Will work for baseball.*

  The time around work and school and baseball gets filled with laundry, cooking, cleaning, puppy training, errands, haggling with the insurance company, and dealing with one of us being sick pretty much all of the time. I watch the housing market, scrolling down the lists of homes that are beyond my reach, and occasionally talk with my realtor about how things are progressing. It's painfully slow.

  Finally, a darling house comes up on Realtor.com that I want to see. It's gray and white, in the school district, in a newer area of town. I set up the appointment and drive across town, parking a few minutes early and watching the ominous clouds gather above the pointed little rooftops. Lightning streaks across the sky, bright and low, visible even in the daylight. The thunder booms overhead as I scope out the quaint neighborhood. A Boston Terrier trots past happily on the sidewalk, past the ornamental grasses. This area is designed for walking, designed for families and kids and pets.

My realtor arrives right on time, but doesn't unlock the house.

"I hate to tell you this but the house just sold. I don't want to show you something and have you fall in love and you can't even put in an offer."

"Wow," I hear myself respond. How are people buying these places so quickly?

"The right place is out there for you guys. We're going to find it," she reassures me. I hear the empathy in her voice, her wanting to transfer optimism and hope to me through her words. I nod, knowing logically it is true but unable to emotionally feel it as my own truth in this moment. My feelings slowly numb with the exception of disappointment and bewilderment. I clear my mind and practice acceptance. Until one accepts what is, there is no moving forward, no healing, no growth. This house is sold, and I have to let that sink in and accept it. I thank her and return to my car, taking a moment to redirect my energy.

I sit in the Toyota, in this car that has seen so much, and wait out the twenty minute hailstorm that rips from the skies above. It beats on the car so loudly that I can't even hear the radio. Harley burrows under a blanket on the backseat, covering her head. I stay parked there on the curb, shutting off the windshield wipers because they can't keep up with the deluge of ice and rain falling onto us. I watch the lightning show and white piles of hail balls gathering on the street and try not to look over at the house, at the neighbors, at what might have been.

Chapter 28

God is within her, she will not fall.

Psalm 45:6

For me, a large part of the healing process is not living in the past, and not fantasizing too much about the future. I make efforts every day to be in the moment, to practice contentment with what I have. Yes, there are days that my mind flashes on what we've lost. It's still every day in fact. Last week I spent ten minutes looking for my favorite gray shorts until it finally kicked in that they were left up at our house, not here with us now. Every single day I think of the little ceramic pot Andy made me by hand in Kindergarten. The struggle is present in some way every day. I also have dreamy moments of nesting into a house, making it our own. By the time that happens Andy might be a teenager and the life I'm picturing no longer an option. Both dwelling on the past and obsessing over the future can drive a person mad. In order to have peace, to have happiness, it is critical to take the time to appreciate what is right now, in this very moment. I'm not claiming it is easy, but once mastered, it is life changing. Appreciate right now. Be present right now. Be here now.

In honor of this effort we do our best to settle in to the place we are sharing. We make the most of what we have in this moment. I try not to think too much on what is lost or what I hope will be provided. I try to live in the here and now, practicing mindfulness and gratitude for today. It's the only way to keep sanity intact through something like this, or through anything really.

The attached garage has been converted into a workshop, with large equipment and workspaces against every wall and in the center. Tools line the walls and the faint smell of sawdust reaches me and immediately transports me back to my childhood. I fondly recall being in the garage with Daddy, hammering on scraps of wood, sanding down a bench, handing over various tools that he needed. I could drive a nail at four years old, finish sheetrock by the time I was eight.

I look around the workspace and see many familiar tools: band saw, drill press, skil saw. But there are others. A strange pressing device with a tall metal handle, the end covered in styrofoam, probably to prevent head injury. A table with a big metal roller, huge steering wheel, and canvas sheets. I look around the corner. Potter's wheels line the aisle, and at the end corner rests a brand new gleaming electric kiln. Stainless steel metal drying and storage racks line the center of the space. The smell of the fresh clay is earthy and soothing. I immediately want to get my hands into it, to be in contact with something primitive and raw and unmade.

I begin with pinch pots, which starts with forming wads of clay into perfect spheres. I tap the blobs onto the wedging board, starting with a rounded cube. Then I spank the clay, slapping my palm onto it as it rotates in my other hand. I roll it like play dough around and around, smoothing out any wrinkles with my fingers. Then with my thumb, I press into the center and begin to squeeze the clay, pinching and turning it until a small bowl begins to emerge. There is something therapeutic, healing, about working with your hands. Other cares temporarily float away and the mind can focus on the task at hand. Squeeze, turn, squeeze. Pinch, pinch, pinch. I make sets of nesting bowls with carved designs, tea bag holders, and small plates. Occasionally I glance over my shoulder at the wheels but know that my previous illness and the medications left side effects that will likely hinder being able to use them. Depth perception issues, dizzy spells from watching any spinning motion, loss of balance and hand eye coordination. It's okay, though, I can make childlike pots all I want.

"You know, I can teach you to use those," Dan, our house host, says through a smile one day. He doesn't miss much, and I see the teacher in him even more today.

"Oh, thank you for the offer, and for sharing this amazing space. I'm so grateful. But I don't think I can handle the spinning and I'm pretty uncoordinated right now."

"I see. I once taught a blind student how to center and throw pottery. I never had a student that couldn't do it. I am confident you can learn it. When you are ready."

I thank him, and a bit of optimism seeps into my mind. I would love to learn how to make bowls, vases, plates, anything really. I let the thought float around as I continue to roll out slabs of clay and form it into little trinket holders. I stamp in mandalas, birds, and letters. I keep this up for a few weeks when The Teacher decides to join me in the studio. He sits at the wheel and becomes one with the clay, moving it up and down until a perfect mound is formed. It looks like a big, perfect breast staring up at us. He takes a sponge from a bucket and squeezes out clay water onto it and proceeds to make a beautiful bowl just to tempt me. I compliment the shape, the lines, his grace in creating it. Then I return to my little hand pots, Tommy coming out to make some of his own. We stand side by side in our flannel jammies at the wedging table, turning and working the clay in silence.

The next day I head out to check on our little projects and the beautiful bowl is waiting right on the center of the table, right where The Teacher knows I stand and work. Right where it will push me to put aside my reservations, ignore my challenges, and forge on ahead anyway. I sigh, hands on hips, and stare at it. It just sits there, regal and simple. Fine. Today I will learn to throw.

The Teacher grins as I tell him I am ready. "Of course you are," he says, a knowing gleam in his eye like Mr. Miagi from the Karate Kid. I shake my head, smiling. *Wax on, wax off.* I follow his directions, grabbing a blob of clay and placing it on the scale. I remove it and begin to wedge it, roll it, prep it for the wheel. I sit and place in on the center plate, with The Teacher on another wheel right next to me. I take a deep breath and look over at him. Here we go.

He is able to teach me, despite my vision problems, despite the spinning of the wheel, despite my dizzy spells, despite my having thought it would be too difficult. I close my eyes and just feel how to pull the clay. I create slowly, but I create. I move slowly, but I move. I heal slowly, but I heal. I make a thousand little porcelain gifts in prayer for the recipients, letting the healing energy resonate through me and into the clay. Each little piece is immersed with gratitude and love.

Grieving is a process that is different each time it is experienced. It is additionally complicated by how each person processes the same loss in a different manner. The loss of our home is deeply saddening for me, and I feel the loss on behalf of my boys magnified beyond description. I can't imagine going through this as a child, losing a childhood home, shaking security and normalcy to its core.

To counter this, I continue to try new things. It distracts the flow of thoughts and allows the mind to explore something healthy, something diversionary. I notice a post on social media about a sound bath, and I flag it. I'm not sure what it is, but the photos look like it resembles something related to meditation, yoga, and perhaps the chakras. I try new things not only for me, but for those that I counsel. This might be a great match for me, and if not, it may help me to match it as a therapy to someone else. My cousin reaches out to me after seeing it online and we decide to sign up and check it out together. I research it a bit and learn that the basic concept is that being exposed to specific megahertz of sound waves can be conducive to healing processes. One specific example is that 432 Hz is called the miracle tone and is said to manifest positive energy within the mind and body. I have music files with Tibetan bowls chiming and I find it very soothing, but I haven't experienced them in person.

On a misty, Sunday morning, I gather up a small blanket, throw on some donated yoga pants and a t-shirt, and make my way across town to the little studio hosting today's sound bath. I arrive early and sip on my tea as I wait for my cousin to arrive and for the studio to be unlocked. I roll down the car windows most of the way, breathing in the fresh air. It's an overcast day with a bit of drizzle shrouding the streets, and the cleansing, dense smell of rain helps me to be in the moment. It is important to be aware of our experience, our body, our life that is right now. Soon, the studio's front door is propped open and we are all wandering in and letting our eyes adjust to the dim light.

The interior of the room is industrial, but made welcoming with bamboo flooring and artwork with the chakras adorning the walls. Himalayan salt lamps and subdued lighting set the mood for tranquility. Twelve yoga mats form a semicircle, angled around a series of massive bowls and a gong in the front of the room. We all take off shoes, put down keys, and find our places on the mats. Everyone rustles around and some begin yoga poses.

I find a pad nearest to the glass front door, which the instructor is covering with a thick blanket, pinning it to the wall. I sit down and start to stretch my neck, letting the tension ease out with each gentle pull. I get in a few minutes of this before we are instructed to lie down, get comfortable, and begin to clear our minds and relax our bodies. I do this, eager to give both my mind and body some restorative moments. The room gets darker and I close my eyes, breathing slowly.

Incense wafts around us as I breathe in deep. It's very heady, and my body alerts me that it is too much, too much smoky fragrance. I try to identify the scent but can't. The first bowl chimes, loud and low. I feel it resonate through my head, through my chest. *Bong*. I feel a tickle in my throat, with a slight itching sensation. *Bong*. My eyes water and I suppress the first round of coughing, trying to quietly clear my throat. It doesn't work, and my body turns against me and begins sputtering out little coughs regardless of how hard I try to keep them from escaping. I break a sweat, feeling the coughing fit form a huge wave and begin to take over my entire body. *Bong*. Cough, cough, cough. I wheeze in a breath. Cough. I grab my blanket, wad it up, and press it over my face to muffle the sound of my whooping. Oh boy. Everyone around me is lying peacefully, quietly. Cough. It gets louder and stronger until I am hacking, a deep and disturbing sound. *Bong*. Hack, hack, hack. It won't stop. I have to get fresh air, have to get a cough drop. The car, I have to get out to the car.

I sit up, barking relentlessly now, and reach the door in two steps. I grab the dark curtain to pull it open, forgetting that it has been tacked to the wall. I tug it open to get to the door handle, and the little tacks fly out across the room. *Ping, ping, ping*. I hear them hit in various directions. Still I hack, struggling to get out, sweat and panic covering my body. I get half of my body around the curtain and feel the cold bar of the door on my hand. I push. Nothing.

I hear a loud whisper right behind me. "It sticks. It says push, but pull it open, it's easier." I use my adrenaline to drag the door open about a foot, the metal screeching on the floor. More tacks fly out.

"I'm so sorry everyone," I cough out, mortified for this interruption to their peace. I run out to the car, breathing in the misty air and nearly hyperventilate, coughing it back out. I beep open the passenger door and rummage around what I call my purse but in reality it is a survival pack of epic proportions. Somewhere in the bottom are cough drops, I just know it. My arm is elbow deep in pocket tissues, granola bars, hair bands, and a million other items I have deemed important enough to pack around in this thirty pound satchel. I finally feel the worn and wrinkled paper bag of Ricola throat drops and rip it from my purse. I quickly unwrap one, pop it into my mouth, and frantically turn it over and over in hopes it will dissolve more quickly and bring relief. The cold, damp air helps too. Finally, the hacking fit subsides and I opt to try and return for the rest of the session.

I sneak back onto my mat, relaxing back into the moment. The sound of the bowls is deafening, so much louder than I could have imagined. It's loud to the point of discomfort. Why didn't I bring in my bag? I always carry earplugs, a habit from so many hospital visits and MRIs. I consider options, such as going to the bathroom to grab some tissue to cram in my ears. I scan the room and locate the bathroom. No, no good, I would have to disrupt too many people to get over there. I pull on the strings of my hoodie and opt to twist them into little knobs that I then shove into my ears. It works to partially muffle the sound to a tolerable decibel, and I am then able to concentrate on the vibrations resonating in my brain. Interestingly, the left side is felt much more strongly than the right. The vibrations are supposedly equilateral, but the difference for me is distinct. Much of the nerve damage that occurred impacted my left side more, and my left ear was in a lot of pain during the viral and secondary infections. I can't help but think this is strongly related to the process going on today and that somehow the sound waves are being processed by my brain waves in a fascinating way. I'm not certain what exactly the sound waves are doing, but I sit with my eyes closed and remain open to that which I do not understand, that which I cannot explain, and the possibilities that I do not yet know about.

Chapter 29

God is with you in everything you do.

Genesis 21:22

In the coming months, I obsessively think about the little clay pot Andy made for me in Kindergarten. Maybe because I know that ceramics survive fires. Maybe because he is growing up and I want a tangible piece of his sweet childhood. Maybe because I want to salvage something from the wreckage, to spite the fire and ease my heart from the losses. Maybe because my mind is a stubborn beast and the thought just won't go away. Maybe it's all of these things combined. It eats at me, but other things come first. Work, school, Little League, laundry, migraines, rain, insurance and recovery paperwork, getting groceries, preparing meals, attending medical appointments.

Despite the other distractions, the tiny little brown pot is always in the back of my mind. It's only about two and half inches of crudely pinched clay, yet the sentiment of that piece weighs a million pounds on my heart. It represents a time that I can't get back. It represents a child's pure love. It represents the small things that mean much bigger things. It represents how you make a house a home.

All of those little things will soon be scraped clean when the county comes in to do debris removal. Soon we will be notified that we have one week to try and salvage anything left on the property before the crews arrive to do their work. Their job is to ensure that anything damaged is completely cleared off the lots, and they must remove the foundation and some of the soil beneath it. Their job is to make sure that no part of our house remains at all. I try really hard to think of it as preparing the land for a new home that will bless someone's family in the future.

Eventually I wake up on a random, sunny Monday, just before the heat of late spring arrives. The monsoon rains have temporarily subsided. It is the Monday following Easter Sunday. I slowly sit up in the bed, assessing my level of headache and vertigo today. Minimal, with the chance of lifting completely after some caffeine. Today is the day. I will find that little pot.

I drop the boys at school and make the drive up the hill. It's my second visit to the property, but I have been through parts of Paradise to photograph and document the wreckage two other times, making this my fourth drive back up. It's getting easier, and though the county clean up won't likely happen this month, I am motivated to keep searching for my treasure.

I haul my bag of tools out from the car and observe that there is already noticeable erosion from all of the downpours post fire. This area saw an unprecedented amount of rainfall and flash flooding, sadly following a long, dry summer. The rains didn't arrive in time this year, and ancient civilizations would have believed that the fire was because we somehow angered the gods and needed to work harder to please them with a new temple and sacrificial offerings. We know instead that faulty electrical transformers and bad administrative judgment calls were to blame this time.

I slowly look around at our destroyed property. It is a shock every time, a shock I will never get accustomed to seeing. Heavy, loose soil and debris are covering the driveway. Insects fly around, and I wonder if this is a good sign or not as I hike up toward the house foundation and ashen flooring of rubble. As I stand there and survey the area, I am able to more clearly assess this time, with determination fueling my mind. I scan the layout and analyze where the pot might have landed. I recall reading about an archaeologist who dug through her burned home after the Carr fire. Her directions were to cover a three foot square radius around where you think the item was, the idea being that as furniture falls and the ceilings collapse, items can be flung away from their normal placing. Another option she gave was to start on one end of the foundation and work in rows, completely sifting through each section of the home at a time. I'm on a mission so I go with option one, and estimate the three foot radius.

On the last visit I dug around a few feet north of where the china cabinet had been. The little pot was on that low cabinet, with a small fountain and a picture of the boys. This time I will dig on the south section. I drag away metal remnants of ducting that cover the section, being careful even through work gloves not to cut or puncture my hands. Once an area is cleared of the top debris, work on the next layer of bigger items. I kneel, tossing chards of the heirloom Noritake china set into a pile to clear the area. I scoop down into the ashes with an old, borrowed garden cultivator with three tines. It's worn wooden handle is strong and warm in my hand. Scoop, scoop, scoop. I scoot my body over six inches and scoop again. I repeat this process one thousand times.

I feel the sweat begin to form on my brow, and with it the trickle of doubt that I won't find it, or it will have broken like everything else, and that finding it in pieces will make me feel even worse than I do right now. Finding it broken will mean that there is no hope left that it might be here, might still be intact. I let the thought escape my mind, because I am in no condition to imprison doubts and fears and what ifs within my own self. They are destructive, weakening forces that should not be allowed to drain valuable energy. Instead I focus on the warmth permeating my head and back, and on the purpose set out before me. Have faith, perseverance, and keep seeking. I continue to dig and scoot over, dig and scoot over.

And then, *scoop, clink*. I know it before I even see it. I am using The Force. I gently pull up the tool, it's worn metal tines balancing something hard and heavy amongst the damp clump of ashes. I let the ashen pile gently roll off of the cultivator and onto the top layer of debris and carefully reach my gloved hand into the soft mound. I feel it immediately, its thick walls familiar in my hand. I brush off the ash and dirt, scooping out a small crystal and more debris from its center. The color is different, darker, and the glaze has little cracks all around it. But it is here, intact and solid, back in my hands. Victory surges through me, quiet and fierce. I take a moment to just hold it, to let the relief leave my body. To be grateful that my obsessing can ease up now. To be grateful that I have this one little thing, this one piece of the past, this memento of a precious gift from my child.

I inspect it carefully, looking for any little cracks or chips in the ceramic. There are none. I hadn't remembered the clay stamping that he had pressed into it, a simple flower shape adorning the outside. As I scrape out more ash from the inside, I see that the flower stamp is also pressed into the interior base of the pot. I immediately recognize that this is something I would do and love that my son at such a young age carries pieces of me within him. I love that his hands worked this clay into a form, that he made it with love for his Mommy. I turn it over, and see his name carved into the bottom. Andy.

I carefully pack it up into the car, trying three different methods because now that I have it I can't let harm reach it. After it is triple packed and wedged safely on the car floor, I then walk around the remains again, able now to scope out the garage and loft area. I bend over and find one of my favorite Christmas ornaments, a hand blown glass angel, paper thin and stripped of the golden paint that had adorned the wings and robe. But it is intact, with the metal hanger attached, and not one chip or crack. How is that possible? I hold it, looking around the area. I carefully run the tool though the ash and right there on top are pieces of my porcelain nativity. I find the star, Mary, and baby Jesus. I dig all around, but find nothing else. No manger, no animals, no Joseph.

I inspect Mary, and the porcelain is lightly tarnished from the burns, but her face is white and unmarred. None of the items are chipped. And the tiny swaddled baby Jesus, so help me, has not one mark or blemish. The purity of the clay was not compromised at all. It looks brand new. I hold the little piece out, tiny and white and pure, in my sooty, ash covered hand. It gleams in the sunlight and represents all that is greater than I am, all that is eternal and can't be burned away, all that is hope and faith and love.

Chapter 30

> So be truly glad. There is wonderful joy ahead, even though you have to endure many trials for a little while.
>
> 1 Peter 1:6

The boys and I continue to cram into the queen sized bed every night, continue to say our prayers, and continue to try and make our situation positive. As the months accumulate, so does the stress of living in close quarters in a space that should be temporary but feels like the walls of permanence are closing in. Our house host struggles with the inescapable realities of living with a pre-teen child, which causes the anxiety level to spike on multiple occasions. None of us could have seen this coming.

Andy can be obnoxious toward me, and toward his brother, which in my mind is to be expected of a twelve year old. I also consider all that he is going through, and it can't be easy to try and become an older version of yourself amidst hormones, constantly being asked to settle down, and having zero privacy. We live by another's rules, in another's home, and the stress of it begins to wear on us all. Our house host, Dan the Teacher, has to share his space with an entire family, compromising the peaceful oblivion the house once had. Andy's behavior isn't off the charts by any means, but in the eyes of our host it is a trigger that causes extreme fight or flight. After receiving a message that the situation wasn't working out for him, I know that our time is limited at best. He can't tolerate Andy challenging me, and is extremely sensitive to behaviors that, though they don't trigger me, require that I begin to regulate them because it is his house.

The message from Dan does trigger me however, and it panics me, primarily because we have exhausted all of our viable resources. My mom has offered for us to stay with her, but they still have no water and are housing three adults, all crammed into a tiny house, with others staying on the property in trailers. It would have to be a last resort. In fact, relocating would likely happen first, because at least we could have water and a more permanent residence. It would mean that we completely start over without a school district, without friends or family nearby, without an income source. If it were only me, I would already be gone. But it isn't just me, it's my boys too. I have fought so hard to give them a stable environment of their same friends, friends met in elementary school that remain friends for life. I had that growing up, and the friendships are like no other, enduring for decades past high school graduation.

Their school, their friends, teachers, and coaches, have been the one consistent factor throughout this disaster. They have been able to see familiar faces, to laugh and be comfortable and to hang out and just be kids again, if only for a while. It freaks me out to think about taking this away too, the one piece of normalcy within their days. Tommy is probably young enough and social enough to start over, but Andy may just retreat inward and not come back out.

I call our insurance company to see what other housing options are available to us. The agent looks into it and lets me know that we could try to secure a hotel for thirty days. One month only. It's just not enough time. I consider staying at the hotel for that month, to give our host a break, but it seems like another major upheaval for the boys, for me, yet again.

I consider buying a trailer and having it as our temporary setup, but one huge problem is that the money would then be tied up and unable to be used for a house if one presents itself. I'm going to need every dollar possible to secure us a place of our own. I call all of the apartment complexes again, asking for updates. They are finally adding to their waitlists after months and months. One complex has seen a drop in the waitlist from fifty to fifteen, which means things are beginning to settle down. I add it to the list of possibilities, but it isn't within the school district. And to be honest, if we are looking at having to switch schools, we might as well just move out of the area, to somewhere with more housing options, less price gouging and desperation, and more ocean waves.

I talk over the predicament with the boys, family, and trusted colleagues. Everyone is in agreement that Andy can try to be on his best behavior, but in reality is still a child. A child that has been through a major trauma, displacement from home for months and months, and now, the beginnings of puberty in very close quarters every day. Each person suggests I have a heart to heart with Dan, hoping that he can manage to deal with the situation for just a bit longer, at least until summer arrives in a few weeks in hopes that more housing options become available. I'm skeptical, only because it is his home, not ours, and I see firsthand how upset he becomes over any type of conflict. The situation isn't fair for him or for us. Any way you spin it, it just isn't fair.

That night, I sit propped up in bed as my head throbs with a migraine. The pain is so overwhelming I can barely form a coherent thought. I manage to pry myself out from under the boys and the dog and make it to the bathroom before the vomiting begins. As awful as the process is, the vomiting is often a sign that the migraine will be over soon.

Sitting on the cool floor with my head resting on the toilet seat, I will things to get better. With my health, with our recovery, with our living situation. It all has to get better. I press a cool, wet washcloth to my face and over the sound of my groans of pain I hear it. Faint, low, and floating in through the window. I use the toilet to pull myself upright and crane my neck to try and see out through the screen. The window is on the second floor and all I can see are leaves from the palm trees and a few stars winking in the night sky. But I hear them, and there is no mistaking that it is the sound of the snow geese flying nearby, calling out and soothing my worried, weary soul.

Chapter 31

As for me and my house, we will serve the Lord.

Joshua 24:15

Eight Months Later

Today is a momentous day, a day representative of good things to come. I am a combination of many emotions and sensations: excitement, nervousness, a bit nauseated, hopeful, determined, grateful. Mostly grateful. I have worked for weeks on a scavenger hunt for the boys. They both have sharp minds that love puzzles, clues to find in riddles, and mystery to solve. Today's hunt will be a challenge for all of us, and I can't wait to get started on it.

I find an old baseball and attach worn, printed parchment paper to it. One side reads," Play some ball; this starts it All." On the other side is a compass and the words," Find your Way back home." while the boys are at the movies, I get everything ready for the hunt, driving around town to place clues for them to find. Finally it is all set up, and I pick up the boys and tell them that I need to look for a lost bracelet at the site of the last game.

Both boys play Little League and most games are at the local Elks Lodge. We head over there and scope it out, under the false pretense that we are looking for a bracelet, though my master plan is for them to find the baseball with the first clue. Tommy spots it first and shows it to me, and Andy immediately comes up to read the inscriptions. We vote to follow the instructions and play some ball. We run back across the parking lot and grab the ball bags from the back of the car.

They pitch, hit, and catch with me in the already hot afternoon heat. I watch my boys round first, second, third, and tag home plate. I eventually make it there and stop on the plate to wheeze myself back to life. Too many months of recovery. Too many months out of shape. But I'm here, playing ball with my loves.

"Now what?" I ask them, still panting. They aren't sure what to do from here, and they begin to discuss it as Andy walks over out of habit to brush off the plate with his hands. The next clue is hidden under the layer of fine dirt. He peels off the clue and carefully wipes off the silt that covers it. It reads, "The advantage is ours and this is the test: Here we gather to work, play, and Rest." We scan the area which is completely deserted. They need to find the next clue soon because it is already crazy hot. I can feel the sun permeating my dark hair and pale scalp. They get it quickly, and I am grateful because I am literally freckling as we speak. In the dugout for the home team the next clue is posted. "Seek those who risk their lives each day, for they can help you find your Way."

We are close to the local fire station, home of our heroes and defenders of this city. I prompt the boys, "What does this mean? What are we looking for next?" The suggestions fly, but Tommy decides at last on the fire station down the street. We hop back in the car and drive. At the station, Andy finds the next clue. It reads, "The date is the same as an urgent Call; the next clue rests upon the wall." Near this fire station is a tribute to 9/11, and the lives lost while saving others. We walk over to it, a piece of the Twin Towers on display. I clearly remember that day, watching the towers fall in slow motion, and it strikes me that everyone I spoke to when it happened just wanted to be home. Home with their loved ones, hugging their children, giving extra kisses at bedtime. Post disaster, people just want to go home.

Tommy grabs the next clue. We go on like this for over an hour, hunting, crazed, and I love every second of it. Their eyes are sharp and I can see their minds working, turning over each clue in their minds, thinking it through. We travel across town and back following the clues and our path to the unknown. After more searching the boys find a flowering plant in a container at Home Depot with the next clue attached to it. "I am many things, but today, I am the Way." This one takes longer, but they eventually figure out that it might be a street. Andy puts it into GPS and we take off, excitement coursing through me. We find the road and I pull over. On the street sign is the next little clue. "It leads to dark if you turn right. Go opposite, and follow the Light." We head up the street and see a chalk sunshine in the middle of the road. We follow the light yellow chalk arrows up the road and to the corner. A math problem waits down on the cement next to a piece of chalk. The clue is staked in the nearby grass and reads, "Trust Me, you must solve for X." They get to solving it and I know we are close. My heart races and the butterflies in my stomach feel more like wild squirrels as they write it out and come up with a solution.

They double check the calculation and agree on the answer. Tommy is certain that it is a house number. We walk to the address and try to decide where the next clue would be, hanging back on the sidewalk. The boys are hesitant to approach an unknown house. Tommy finally gets up the courage to ring the doorbell. We wait, but no one opens the door. They decide it is safe to look around more closely and find the clue under the doormat. It reads, "There is no key, just these clues Three:

1. Zero to the power of zero
2. The three that follow the One
3. The most powerful force in the universe
Combine these all and you have found your Way.

They talk, and work, and solve. We get the numbers arranged and move on to the last step. What is the most powerful force in the universe? The boys are obsessed with the nature channel, always watching tornadoes and lightning and space documentaries. Water can cut through mountains. Wind can blast a path through any town in the Midwest. And we know firsthand what fire can do. Yet what is stronger than all of these? Tommy answers, "God."

"Yes, and what is God? Why are we here and what are we supposed to do?" I ask them. We think on this, because it is the age old question of the meaning of life and all the great minds have pondered it for thousands of years. We have it figured though. "Love," we all agree.

"Okay, bring it in for a family hug and let's generate some love around us." We all move in tight and I swear I can feel that force field of energy around us, protecting and guiding. We join hands and step toward the doorway.

"Don't break the chain," I tell them as we stretch arm in arm. Andy, Tommy, and then me. I take a deep breath, and say, "Okay, Andy, enter the passcode and see what happens."

He looks like he is considering the ethics of this and glances back at us. He never wants to bend any of the rules. "We've come this far, so go ahead," I tell him, smiling.

"Dude, just go for it," Tommy nudges him closer.

"Okay," Andy says and I hear the code beep into the keypad. The electric gear turns and we hear the lock click open. And this is the moment.

My mind flies back to putting in an offer on the house and being outbid. I recall getting over the loss of possibilities, again. Going back to the drawing board, again. Squeezing us all into a queen sized bed, again. And then, the call. The glimmer of hope. The higher bidders backed out of the deal. My realtor and I work to make it happen, and I take a giant leap of faith that it will all work out, that this is the place God has planned for us. It feels right, but also like a huge decision, a huge responsibility to take on all by myself. I take the plunge and sign all the papers.

I flash back over memories of the past two months of tearing up old pet damaged flooring, painting over pink and lavender walls, cleaning and scrubbing and scouring off years of residue until the stove gleamed. My thumbs are still peeling and tender from all of the work. Volunteer crews of guys busted out old tile, replaced the floors, filed into the garage to assemble piece after piece of furniture. Friends and family showed up to help roll fresh paint onto the walls. Coaches donated time and money to get debris hauled off and hire professional help when we needed it for projects.

Facebook donations from around the globe after the fire helped with the financial efforts needed to secure us a place. Donations made by strangers all over the world to the Salvation Army funded a washer and dryer and some furniture. Local churches and companies donated mattresses and other basic household needs. Individuals donated new and gently used items such as pillows, blankets, toiletries, games, and gift cards. So many hands, so many prayers, and so much love made this house a possibility for us. And the boys are about to see it for the first time. They don't know it yet, but we are home.

Epilogue

The boys and I are still forming a human chain, standing outside of the house they have never seen, with me at the end holding on tight as the door swings wide open. Andy steps over the threshold and we all shuffle in single file, hand in hand, into the entryway. None of us breathe.

Today is the day, today is the start of many starts, the beginning of the new beginning, again. Of all the many start overs during the past year, this one so far is my favorite. I blink rapidly several times. We are finally here. It doesn't yet feel familiar, doesn't have our stamp or our memories or our love yet. But it will. We have photos to hang, artwork to create, memories to make, meals to cook, hugs and kisses and owies to be had, prayers to pray, movies to watch, popcorn to pop, pajamas to wear way into the afternoon, dancing moves to bust, brownies to bake, cuddles to appreciate, and time to share as a family. Me and my boys, and little Harley. We will make this house our home.

I squeeze their hands one last time before letting them look around. They hesitantly turn away to explore, to peek down the hall and try to understand what is happening. Andy is on to me, and turns to ask what is going on. I can see it all over his face. He knows. Before I can respond, Tommy runs back in and loudly asks, "Mommy, can we buy this house?" He is clutching his hands together so tightly that his little fingers are turning red.

I look at them, and make a disappointed expression, and exaggerate a sad, heavy sigh. "I'm sorry guys, I can't buy this house for you right now."

Andy says nothing, still convinced something is up. He eyes me carefully.

"Is it too expensive? Did it already sell?" Tommy has a thousand questions driven by past disappointments.

"I can't buy this house right now, because, well, the truth is...I already did."

Andy says, "I knew it! I knew something was going on."

"What!" Tommy covers his face with his hands in shock. Then he begins to jump up and down, elated and screaming and running through the house to find his room. They stake their claims, and then we retour the whole house together, trying out the couch and looking in closets. The flooring still isn't done, and we have only one bed for now, but the boys don't seem to care and are over the moon at having a place to call home. I promise to get the floors completed and to get furniture for their rooms as soon as possible.

I take a minute to let it all sink in, deep into my soul. I again give thanks. Over and over, I give thanks. The boys join me in the dining room, and we hug tightly, sealing the past, present, and future between us. We say a prayer of thanks and ask for our new home to be blessed from above. I know already that it is. The boys look up at me, and with more love in my heart than I could ever have imagined, I lean down, kiss their sweet heads, and softly tell them, "We got this."

Chapter 32

Introduction to Coping Techniques

Each of us has our own unique set of experiences, perceptions, and personality traits that make up who we are. Because of this I always offer students and clients a variety of coping techniques to try out, assess their effectiveness, and then modify as needed. We all know that despite our best efforts to avoid it, stressors will happen. We each need a plan in place now for stressors that will occur later on. Trying to formulate a plan during a high stress moment is really ineffective, and this is exactly why we don't want to wait to have an action plan in place until stress occurs. If you can determine now what works for you ahead of time, it will help you to work through the difficult moments that lie ahead.

Stress builds up over time and along with traumas, can have a destructive cumulative impact on our health. This means that one stressor is manageable, two are more challenging, and multiple stressors are really difficult to navigate through. Current traumas can bring up issues with past traumas, making us feel victimized or weakened or unstable all over again. The good news is that your coping tools are also cumulative. You have strengths that have helped you through rough times in the past and those can absolutely be used again, even if the situation is completely different.

Included in this chapter are a selection of strategies that can be used to help with symptoms of PTSD, anxiety, depression, and to counter stressors in general. Some of these include exercise, grounding, meditation, prayer, mindfulness, music, aromatherapy, and breathing techniques. All of these are supported with empirical research studies showing their efficacy and usefulness in areas such as better sleep, increased immune systems, lower blood pressure, decreased heart rate, lower anxiety, reduced pain, and higher levels of life satisfaction.

When possible, try out new techniques and evaluate how they work for you personally. I recommend that the techniques be tried out during better days when your body and mind are under less intense stress if it is possible. I have my students and clients try at least three from the list and then rank them on a Likert-type rating scale of 1-10 for each one's helpfulness. (1 is very ineffective; 10 is highly effective). By determining a numeric value, it helps to reinforce in our memories which strategies to use again during the tough moments. You might consider making a list of the strategies that work best in order to help you recall what to do when your symptoms are intense.

I also recommend trying them more than once in order to accurately determine how well each one works, or doesn't, for you as an individual and for where you are at this point in dealing with whatever is on your plate. As you try them, keep an open mind. Keep practicing those that work for you as part of your plan to reduce the effects of stress in your life. Keep in mind that these exercises and techniques are not intended to replace the guidance of a mental health professional. Please seek help if you need it.

Past Traumas

It sometimes seems like trauma after trauma or challenge after challenge is designed to beat us down. But what if the opposite is true? What if you take time to identify what you have been through and begin to view yourself as the badass warrior that you really are? If a friend had been through your life, what would you say to encourage him or her? You would very likely point out strengths of character and be able to find words like amazing, strong, determined, and resilient. My challenge to each of you is this: be that friend that sees the strengths, and be that friend to yourself. Take a look at a difficult time and analyze from an outside, non-judgmental, loving way, how you got through it. With each positive word you find, hang on to that tightly because they are the same characteristics that will get you through everything else.

This experience of life on Earth will be a series of difficulties, just as it is a series of blessings. If you can learn to be your own cheerleader and pack around a tool belt of ways to deal, it will get easier. The hard times don't disappear from your path, but the ways through them are much, much better with tools. I will share an example of how this works.

One of my clients came to me in crisis after the fire. I remember her clearly repeating, "I don't know how to do this."

"But you might," I said.

She looked at me through her tears, confusion all over her face. "I haven't been through this before. I don't know how to do it. I've never been through anything like this. I'm lost."

"Okay. Let's put the fire experience aside for now. Think back over your life prior to that. Find a really difficult time and tell me briefly about it."

She knows immediately what to discuss. I see it in her face as soon as she remembers the past experience. She describes a time many years before, when she was in a car accident. She talks about the physical pain, the fear, the long term disability. I ask her to describe herself as if she were talking about a friend. She comes up with some really fantastic words.

"But that was a totally different situation," she repeats.

"Yes, but what you did to get through that can be applied to now. What did you do back then? Where did you find your strength?"

She then proceeds to tell me about her breathing techniques, meditation and yoga, and music therapy. I point out that all of those can still be practiced, and should be practiced. We go over self-care, personal support systems, and some extra exercises for anxiety. It all hits her and I see it happen. "I'm actually kind of a badass," she tells me.

"Not just kind of," I respond.

"Yeah, that's true." She smiles, feeling better knowing that she has a plan in place for where to start with putting her life back together again.

The moral of this story is that you do have skills that have gotten you to this point, even if this point is completely different and foreign. Apply what you already know, remember what worked for you in the past, and tailor it to today's challenges. Incorporating some of the following strategies will help as well.

Acceptance

Before we can begin to problem solve and find our way out of the puzzle, we have to assess our situation. You can't climb over a wall if you can't accept that you are facing a wall. You can't escape quicksand if you think it is something else. As hard as it is to accept bad situations, we all experience them and accepting whatever is going on is the first step to dealing with it. It doesn't mean you have to like it. It doesn't mean it is fair, or right. It doesn't mean that no one made a mistake that just tore your life to shreds. It just means that to get through it, you need to know what it is. Then you can make a plan of attack for dragging yourself out.

We all need time after loss to get through the shock and pain, which will slowly begin to change. If you are experiencing an inability to face what is happening, remember to be kind to yourself and practice as much self-care and other coping skills as much as possible. There were times when all I could do was practice the breathing techniques, so that is what I did. Allow yourself to get through the shock, tend to basic needs such as shelter, water, food, and sleep, and once those are met you will be able to better assess what the situation is. Eventually you will have to face the situation, such as when I had to drive back up that hill. But I gave myself time to feel stronger, to take care of more pressing issues, before facing what I knew would be a really difficult journey through destruction. Work on preparing yourself to be grounded in order to face what you need to get done.

Identify any Triggers

Surviving a traumatic event doesn't end with the event itself. It can be a continued survival, a continued fight for regaining normalcy and peace. Post-Traumatic Stress is very common after a life threatening event such as the Camp Fire and its ripple effects on our community. It is wise to be aware of potential triggers that may exacerbate your condition. Someone offered me a free Airbnb right after the fire. "Come get away in a mountain resort up in the pines." Um, no thank you. Tall pines still freak me out. If being around something results in worse symptom levels, evaluate what you can tolerate so that you don't negatively impact your recovery. For triggers that we cannot predict, such as seeing something on television or hearing something outside that vividly reminds us of an event, it is proactive to be aware of how triggers impact us and to have a preparedness plan in place.

My personal plan is to practice my breathing techniques and to briefly remove myself from the situation if possible. Moving outside for some fresh air helps my breathing and gratitude exercises. Knowing this means that even if I am caught off guard, I have an action plan to help alleviate the stress of seeing something that takes me back to that fateful day. Some people plan to call a friend or loved one to distract themselves or even stay on the phone through a panic attack. Some people pop in earbuds and listen to soothing music or a book. There are endless choices for you to consider. Again, make a plan now before the trigger occurs.

Think of it as packing a survival kit or loading up a tool box; you want those items with you before you actually need them. Then, when the time comes and you are faced with a trigger affecting you, you will have what you need to better deal with the situation.

Physical Exercise

When we move our bodies during exercise, amazing things happen that we don't even feel. Our brains signal for the release of happy hormones, which counter stress, increase immunity, and fight off depression and anxiety. In addition, exercise is great for releasing pent up emotions that may not otherwise have a healthy outlet. In order to balance out the mental and emotional stressors we encounter, our bodies need to move to generate the endorphins that will boost our moods and overall health. Breaking a light sweat is ideal; you will know that happy chemicals are being released and that toxins are being flushed out. Not all exercise has to be intense, though, as a peaceful walk or gentle stretching can also reduce anxiety and make us feel better during stressful times. The key is to find what works for you, and to keep doing what works. Perhaps pushups or squats work for you throughout the day. Maybe you do stretches a few times a day, or each morning, or before bed. Maybe a run works, or brisk walking, lifting weights, swimming, or Tai Chi. You can use a set time or just use impromptu mini exercises when you feel you need it. The important thing is to remember to make the time, even if it is only for five minutes to quickly recharge your body and mind.

As you exercise, try to clear your mind of stressors, problems, and negative thoughts. Use the time to focus on your body, the feel of moving your muscles, and your breathing. Give thanks for the health you have, even if it is not ideal. Be grateful for the body you have, and its ability to keep you going. Encourage yourself to keep moving, to keep feeling what your body can do. This will make the time spent exercising also act as an emotional strengthening, pairing mind and body together in order to heal the spirit. As you move, be in the moment physically, which will help you both mentally and emotionally.

Gratitude

Practicing gratitude has immensely powerful healing properties. Studies on gratitude exercises have shown that people who reflect on being grateful and feel a sense of gratitude report less pain, less illness, more joy, and have increased resiliency against difficult times. There is something that occurs with feelings of gratitude, and a grateful mindset, that arms us against all that is threatening to bring us down. We can all use a big dose of this antidote, so here are some gratitude exercises for you to try.

<u>Gratitude Jar</u>

Find a jar, or box, or bowl and set it out where you see it throughout the day. Each day, write down something that makes you feel grateful onto a small piece of paper. Holding the paper, take a moment to focus on how your body feels with gratitude inside it. Let it expand into you, and fill your body and mind. Once you have let the physical sensation of gratitude occur, put the paper in the jar. Over the course of the month, your jar will become full of little reminders that there are good things to reflect upon in your life, and the process of doing so will make you stronger. One great thing that I really like about this exercise is that the collection of gratitude papers can also serve to boost your mood and mindset on particularly rough days. If you are feeling down, dump out all of the little grateful thoughts and read them one at a time, putting them back as you go. Remember that when you read them, you need to pause to actually *feel* them. Gratitude should result in a physical response if we focus on it and let it happen. This physical response results in the release of hormones that will help to stabilize emotions and our body chemistry.

Feeling exhausted, overwhelmed, angry, or sad is a normal part of dealing with the aftermath of a natural disaster. On days that you are struggling to identify things that spark gratitude, you can use this list of prompts to reflect on possible topics for your jar. Your reflections do not have to be in the present tense; you can remember a time when you were particularly grateful or you can recall a wonderful memory that you are grateful to have. Try your best to physically feel grateful or thankful for what you have experienced in your life.

<u>Gratitude Prompts</u>
A person in your life
A special memory
A love you felt
A friendship
A meaningful place
An item that you have
A unique experience in your life
Something that makes you smile or laugh
Something fun you did
Something beautiful you saw
Something you can see right now
Something you can taste
Something wonderful you ate
Something you can hear
Something you have learned
Something you have taught
A good book you have read
A movie you have seen
Something shared
Something that brings you comfort
Basic needs being met (food, shelter, sleep)

This is an abbreviated list; you can find longer lists online by searching for "gratitude prompts."

This Too Shall Pass

Knowing that your situation is temporary is a key component of getting through it. If we can focus on just getting through bits of it at a time it helps immensely. If you allow yourself to consider the overwhelming totality of circumstances and their potential consequences all at once, your sanity will be compromised. I once heard an old and wise question, "How do you eat an elephant?" This is an interesting thought to consider when faced with something huge that you have no idea how to get through. The answer: one bite at a time. With trauma, disaster, and grief, it isn't about taking it one day at a time. A whole day can feel really overwhelming. It's often getting through moments at a time. And this is a good strategy to use when things are really rough. Concentrate on just getting through little pieces at a time.

Once you have your time divided up, and you have committed to getting through the next 30 seconds or two minutes or one hour or one week, you need to have ways to pass the time with healthy strategies. This is where deep breathing, imagery, music therapy, or any of the other techniques presented here can be helpful. Hobbies are also an immense tool, though I know it is extremely challenging to resume them immediately after a loss of home. It took me months to be able to collect some yarn and crochet hooks, essential oil kits, and beads for jewelry. And even longer to collect the energy and motivation to make something. But I did listen to eBooks, took walks with my kids, and played with the dog. I bought some new music and tried out new online music stations. I let friends have us all over for dinner so that I could just hang out and be around something normal for an evening and not have to cook or clean up. Other times I would do laundry, or clean out my car; these tasks felt productive and gave me a sense of immediate gratification that the task was done and helped harder moments to pass.

Have your set of strategies at the ready and face whatever time frame you have set with those techniques. 30 seconds of breathing. Two minutes of gratitude. Five minutes of stretching. Ten minutes of walking outside. One week of all of these. One month of these plus something new each week. As time passes and you continue these strategies, you will grow stronger. Your challenges will be faced with more resiliency, your fears with more ability to push them out of your way, your pain with the knowledge of how to get through it.

Meditation

Meditation does not have to be a formal process or even look like a traditional meditation might look. This can simply be a practice of clearing and silencing your mind. There are many resources available such as apps, books, and videos on guided meditations that make it easy for beginners to follow. If possible, note any favorites and bookmark them or commit them to memory to use when needed. I get outside near moving water whenever I can and the soothing sound helps to clear my mind. When I have to be inside, I use nature sounds and meditation music to keep my focus on my breathing and off of the little mental hamster on the treadmill running amok with my thoughts. And whether in person, on YouTube, or my Amazon music, I love the sound of Tibetan bowls chiming away my stress.

Many people find a walk or hike to a serene or beautiful view is a great way to meditate. Think about the places around you that you might want to access. Once you get there, focus on your surroundings, and then your body. Focus on your breathing and the connection to all living things. Feel your body as it begins to relax. Clear your mind.

The goal of meditation is to gain awareness and to achieve a mentally and emotionally calm and stabilizing state. This is important to do when overwhelmed, making decisions,

coping with grief or stress, or fighting illnesses. Here are the basic meditation steps for beginners:
1. Sit or lie down in a comfortable position. Many people opt to sit with legs crossed and arms resting open on the thighs.
2. Close your eyes, which will help with concentration and awareness.
3. Focus your attention on your breathing and how it feels within your body to inhale and exhale. If you get distracted by your thoughts, return the attention to your breathing.
4. Relax your body and mind. Feel your muscles relax, feel your breathing relax, and allow your mind to be in this moment of relaxation and peace. Music, chants, or nature sounds can help with this.

There are many, many tools for meditation at various levels and with various emphasis on styles or focal points, such as gratitude, compassion, stillness, and energy movement. The list is endless, which means that there is some type of meditation match for everyone regardless of skill level or interests. I recommend trying several and practicing them to discover what works best for you.

Prayer

Regardless of your beliefs, if you believe in something bigger than yourself, if you have faith, religion, or spirituality, it can be a powerful tool to help you through tough moments. Using prayer or spirituality exercises can strengthen your connection to either God or to the energies in the universe. Prayer is especially effective during high stress times. A memorized prayer can help to focus on something outside of ourselves. Remember to be easy on yourself if you don't recite it all or completely. Our minds may not function at the highest capacity when we are experiencing anxiety. During those times, some people simply invite or ask for comfort and try to focus on that connection. For those of you who read the previous chapters of this book, you know that The Lord's Prayer is one that I memorized years ago and that I have shared this gift with my children. If you are ever unsure of how or what to pray, this particular prayer is a great one to be familiar with. I also want to mention that prayer does not have to be a formal process. I often have time with God throughout my day. Prayer can be sending a grateful thought for what you have, or a request for strength to get you through the day, or just taking a moment to connect and allow yourself to feel comforted or calmed. Be open to what prayer can be for you as an individual to deepen your relationship with God and help to reinforce that we are not alone.

Energy Focus

Clap your hands vigorously three times. (If you don't want to disturb anyone you can omit the claps). Then rub your hands together as quickly and firmly as you can for about ten seconds. Notice the heat beginning to form. Keeping your hands pressed together, feel the energy in them and direct it to the rest of your body or to the one spot that needs attention. Don't separate your hands until the energy has moved out of them. Once it is gone, you may repeat as needed. If you want to pair it with a mantra to say or think, consider: With this energy I am strengthened. Or: With this energy, I am healed. Even better, create a mantra of your own that is meaningful. The point of this exercise is to focus your energy where it is needed and to have some control over where it goes. This technique can also help to reduce anxiety symptoms.

Grounding

Grounding is a method of mind or thought distraction used to manage overwhelming emotions such as grief, panic, anger, and anxiety. There are many exercises to choose from which help us to pull out of a state of extreme emotions or feeling overwhelmed by deliberately switching our mental focus. These exercises move our mind back into our bodies and the present moment, giving us a sense of stability. Grounding is related to mindfulness and is very effective in countering anxiety and other symptoms by creating a calming effect on the body. It is receiving recognition for its use in helping those with PTSD, which can occur from many traumatic events, including accidents, sudden illness, and loss. Regardless of your level of trauma or anxiety, grounding has much to offer in the areas of coping, healing, and moving through difficult times.

The point of grounding is to utilize your sensory perceptions to connect you with the here and now as opposed to allowing our emotions to take over. By concentrating on one or a combination of our five senses, we regain control of our focus. Additionally, grounding can go beyond our five senses and serve to connect us to higher energies and foster greater spiritual growth. Ideally, you will want to try out several different exercises and find out what works for you, modifying or combining methods as needed. It's a good strategy to have several to choose from, because each reaction to your situation may be different and what works one day might not be as effective on another day. By having a collection of several or more options, you will be more confident in being able to manage powerful emotions and find the grounding exercise that fits the moment.

<ins>Grounding Exercise 1</ins>

Place your feet shoulder width apart. Slowly rock back onto your heels, pressing them firmly into the ground. Pause there for a moment, just feeling your heels balance you and connect you with the ground. Return your feet to flat. Then slowly roll up onto your toes or the balls of your feet, again pressing firmly into the ground. Pause there before returning your feet to flat. Now, slowly rock to balance on the outer edges of your feet, concentrating on balance and gentle pressure into the ground. Return to flat. Lastly, roll your feet inward to balance on the inner ridge of your feet. Return to flat, and repeat as needed. This particular exercise can be done standing or sitting, and can be done quietly anywhere.

The great thing about grounding is that you can pair it with other techniques to boost effectiveness. One boost is to pair it with breathing; breathe in while feet are flat, focusing on pulling in positive and calming energy, and breathe out while pressing into the ground, exhaling stress, negativity, or pain and pushing those into the ground with your feet. The order of heels, toes, or sides does not matter, so it's not necessary to remember it in a certain pattern. If you are unable to use your feet for this exercise, you can also use your hands in the same manner on any hard surface, or at the same time with your feet.

Grounding is basically the process of getting centered within your own body, and you don't have to just use your feet in order to accomplish it.

Grounding Exercise 2

There are many exercises designed to use sensory stimulators, such as touching something very cold, holding something warm, tasting something tart, sweet, or spicy, petting an animal, identifying every color in the rainbow, closing your eyes and hearing all the sounds, even calling a friend to decompress. These exercises help to ground you back into your body by focusing on a physical stimulation rather than focusing on thoughts, fears, or external stressors. Find something sensory to experience, and be in the moment with that sensation.

Earthing

Earthing is the process of putting bare skin into contact with the earth, or soil. It is grounding, both literally and figuratively. There are many potential benefits from this form of grounding, including reducing inflammation, stress, pain, and improving sleep and immune systems. Our bodies are electrical, and so is the Earth. It makes sense that we can and should benefit from that connection. Our shoes, made with rubber soles, break that connection by blocking the flow of electricity back and forth between our feet and the ground. While soil is thought to be the most effective, you can also ground on rocks, sand, grass, and even cement, though I recommend the natural options when possible.

Contact with the ground can have a calming effect both physically on the nervous system, and psychologically, helping to regulate emotions. Additionally, soil contains healthy bacterium or soil microbes, which are thought to stimulate the production of serotonin in our bodies. Serotonin is the body's natural antidepressant and a critical neurotransmitter. Healthy levels can significantly improve memory, mood, sleep, appetite, and behavior.

One of the best ways to accomplish contact with the Earth is to simply go outside without wearing your shoes or socks and get the soles of your feet into direct contact with soil. When I was really ill, I couldn't just walk around soaking up all the Earth's electrons, so I had to modify the concept to fit my needs. Instead of walking, I would sit with my bare feet on the ground every chance I got. At Little League games, I would wear flip flops so that I could easily have my feet on the grass while I watched my boys play. I still like to sit and place my hands on the earth when I hike and take a break. Remember that you need to have two points of contact (skin to earth), so engage both feet or both hands so that the energy can have a path of travel, in and out.

Laughter

Stress builds up in our bodies and we have to be conscientious about letting it release. One way to fight the toxic chemicals of stress is to produce more healthy chemicals. It can be challenging to try and laugh during difficult times, but I can't emphasize enough how important this is to our brains and bodies. I don't always have time to sit and watch a funny movie, or even a half hour long sitcom. But my kids and I always make time to watch a few YouTube videos of funny animals, pranks, or mishaps. The fact that cats get scared of cucumbers makes me laugh every time I see it. Even during grief, especially during grief, it is important to try and find humor and laughter. This will release endorphins that can relieve stress and lessen pain, and will help to maintain healthy neuropathways in the brain.

Music

Music therapy can serve a variety of purposes, and one of its primary benefits during loss and grief is that it provides a distraction of the mind. Focusing on the sounds of something outside of ourselves can significantly help. Certain songs can also boost mood, which is an important tool during tough times. I recommend having multiple playlists to use for a variety of moods. For example, my playlists include Tibetan chimes for meditation and calm, water sounds for stress or to help with sleep, and pop music to boost my mood. I also like some classical and jazz, which I use for creativity. I always carry an extra pair of earbuds in my bag so that I can access music (or my audio books) whenever needed. This came in especially handy while waiting for hours at a time at the FEMA Disaster Recovery Services appointments.

Visualization

Using a visualization technique can help to redirect symptoms of PTSD and lower anxiety levels. The image of something calming and beautiful that you can easily picture in your mind will help to divert negative thought patterns to a safe place in your mind, and then from there you can decide where you want to focus your thoughts and energy. There is a specific trick to this though, which is very important. The image has to be chosen prior to the anxiety occurring. The way to begin this strategy is to pick a calm moment when you can concentrate and focus. Do a few cleansing breaths or shake out your muscles to relax. Think of a place, time, or thing that brings you serenity, or peace, or joy. It needs to be something you can very easily "see" when you close your eyes or imagine it. Practice seeing it, and with that, focus on the calming effect it has on your body.

If you have access to the internet, YouTube is a great resource for free tools to use in this way. I often play ocean sounds or water and nature sounds, and there are videos with soothing pictures to accompany it. I also use nature outside as a visual, and in particular clouds or the skyline. When I don't have access, I imagine a dock on a calm lake. I picture the grey weathered wood, and think of how it would feel on my bare feet. I think of how the lake and the wet wood would smell, and how the soothing lapping of gentle waves or soft wind would sound. This is the type of image that can stimulate sensory perceptions to divert our mind and body from stress.

Unwanted Thoughts

PTSD and other conditions can create intrusive and unwanted thoughts. This is actually a very common occurrence and can be a hindrance to our healing, concentration levels, and peace of mind. The primary reason these thoughts are so damaging is because they pop in randomly and can be near impossible to dismiss. Most people go about banishing thoughts the wrong way, because the way to actually deal with them is counter intuitive. Most of us by nature simply fight the thought, or feel weakened by it, or don't know what to do so it plays on repeat in our minds over and over. Fighting it does no good. Let me demonstrate: Do not think about a giraffe. Don't picture it eating a tall tree. Now, don't think about that giraffe being purple. With orange polka dots.

I know, you pictured the purple giraffe. You are still thinking about it. This shows that telling our minds to not think of something is ineffective. We can't just not think about certain things. Another example is triggers. Every time I see a huge pine or redwood tree, I think about it being on fire. I can't hear fireworks without thinking about exploding propane tanks. But I don't want those to be able to take over my day, mood, life.

The way through this particular experience is to acknowledge the thought. I take a moment, allow the bothersome thought or emotion to be identified and named, and then I give it permission to leave. Here are some ways you can help to get it out of your mind:

Paper Toss

Envision the thought written down on a piece of paper. Now imagine crumpling it up in your hand, and tossing it into a bright blue recycling bin with a lid that can close. You could alternately put it through a shredder, or picture it on a smart screen and swipe it off. I recommend adapting this technique into something specific that works for you personally. My son pictures his worry on a baseball, throws it up into the air, and smacks it hard with a bat, watching it sail out of the ballpark. Alternately, you can actually write it down on paper and then destroy it, but I have found that if you can master the visualization of this instead it is faster and more convenient.

Replacement Thoughts

We can't control what randomly pops into our heads, especially if those random thoughts are a result of having experienced a traumatic event. But after acknowledging the thought and letting it pass through us, we can decide what we want to spend our energy on. Be prepared with what you would like to focus on instead of what you don't. Decide ahead of time a few thoughts that are worth your time, and will add value to your life, and be ready to concentrate on those in place of negative thoughts or disturbing memories. It doesn't immediately stop the unwanted thoughts, but they will gradually lessen over time. And until they do become less intense and less frequent, you are gaining control over how you let yourself respond to those thoughts.

This is a good time to discuss reaction versus response. When I see a huge pine tree, I react to the image of it on fire. My body sends fear hormones so that I can use fight or flight. My reaction is not one that I choose, it is a survival instinct of my body sensing danger. Even if the danger is perceived and not truly a threat, my body reacts in the same way. What I can choose is how I respond to that impulse. I look at the tree, note that it is not actually on fire, acknowledge that it is an irrational fear as a result of trauma, and then focus on being calm. I opt to let that fear pass through me and pay attention to it leaving my body as I focus on a calm image. My thoughts then turn to my choice of thoughts. Almost always it is gratitude. Gratitude for being here, being alive, having my children safe with me, regaining my health, gratitude for answered prayers.

Our brains are incredibly resilient and able to change in miraculous ways. If a nerve ending doesn't respond or responds intermittently, messages will keep being sent to it until it either repairs itself or is considered permanently non-functioning. When that happens, new nerve branches will form wherever they can and information will be rerouted. What this means is that the brain is very adept at creating new pathways. And the best part? We can choose some of those pathways on our own!

Here is an example of how this works, based on neuroimaging of brains. Our brains create grooves, like those old vinyl records, or like a rivulet from water over time. They create these grooves to help us get to information easily, especially information that we use all the time. This is how we easily recall the alphabet, or names, or certain memories or thoughts. When we get into the habit of thinking something negative or have a recurring reaction to trauma, we easily jump to that thought because of the groove. In order to change that, we have to realize our thought patterns, stop the thought we don't want as it occurs, and redirect it elsewhere. When we do this, new neuropathways will form. New habits of thinking will form. It takes time for those new grooves to deepen, but it can be done; we have the scientific evidence to back it up. Eventually it gets easier and easier to stop the negative thought and access the positive one(s) of your choice. It is in this way that you will take back control of your life.

Reframing
Reframing is a technique that allows us to view a situation or experience in a different way than we were before. I could choose to feel victimized or beat down by losing everything in the fire, or depressed because my long term illness recovery is not as fast or complete as I want it to be. Traumatic events are called trauma for a reason, and I am not claiming that horrific things don't happen. Sadly, they do. But I hope for each and every one of you reading this that you are able to take whatever struggles have been placed before you and begin to reframe them in a way that makes them bearable, and allows them to facilitate growth and healing.

Both the illness and the fire almost killed me. Twice now I have been much closer to death than I like to consider. But I am a better person because of it. A better counselor, a better teacher, a better mother, a better human. I am reframing those awful experiences to use them in a way that helps me to help others. I am more patient, more grateful, more present in the moment each day because of those events. And that is a true gift, an immeasurable blessing sprouting from something dark and painful. I challenge you to look for the good that can one day come from your pain.

Mindfulness
I've described being aware of thoughts and feelings, and identifying those and letting them pass through. This is akin to mindfulness, which is a state of awareness and being in the present moment. I want to share some specifics about

mindfulness and how it can be used as a powerful agent of change in our daily lives. One key element that is essential to successful mindfulness is being non-judgmental while being present. And while this means being non-judgmental toward everyone, I have found it is most relevant when dealing with PTSD to be non-judgmental of yourself. Intrusive thoughts or fears are not a sign of weakness, nor are they indicators that people are better off without us or that we are doing anything wrong. Allow yourself to recognize what you are feeling, so that you can then begin to release it if needed. Continue to do this by practicing being aware of what is around you and what is within you. Incorporate kindness to self and others as a part of being in this present moment.

Breathing

Breathing can be incorporated into mindfulness practices, or used as a solitary technique independent of other coping skills. I pair it with positive thoughts and energy redirection, but even on its own it is proven to have immediate and beneficial results on body, mind, and spirit. Breathing can counter anxiety by lowering blood pressure and pulse rates as a result of stress and can have instant calming effects. This can be yoga breathing, Navy Seal training breathing, abdominal breathing, or relaxation breathing. Call it whatever you want and choose a variety that works best for you.

How to breathe to fight stress:

Before you begin this exercise, imagine that your lungs have a compartment of the most purified air and it is situated just below your belly button. This is the air we want to access. As you breathe in, pull up that air from deep in your abdomen. Always inhale slowly through the nose, pausing briefly to hold each breath, and exhaling out slowly through the mouth. In my classes, I demonstrate with a 3-3-3 count and then instruct everyone to find the number of seconds that works best for the situation and the individual. For example, I use a longer count for getting back to sleep than I do for relaxing during the day. The count is for how many seconds you slowly breathe in, how many seconds you hold your breath, and how many seconds you slowly exhale. Repeat the sequence until you have reached the desired state of calm or relaxation.

I pair the breathing with guided positive self-talk. As I inhale, I think, "I am calm with this breath," or, "I am breathing in positive, healing energy." As I exhale, I think, "I am letting go of negativity," or, "I am cleansing my mind and body." You can choose what you want to say or you can count, or you can just feel the breaths in your body.

Butterfly Hug

This is a technique used along with EMDR therapies, and it works remarkably well to help calm us down when anxiety is really high. Place your hands together like you are making a bird, palms facing you and sliding one hand over the other until your thumbs touch. Move your fingers together like wings. Place your hands in this position on your chest, with your fingers just below or on your collarbones. Slowly lift one "wing" and tap your chest, then tap the other. Continue to tap one side at a time while feeling the taps and feeling the love as you would from a hug. After a few minutes, stop and think about how you feel. If you feel better, you can stop; if you still feel anxious, repeat it as needed. This is intended to help you get through moments of overwhelming emotion, which can come on in waves or hit unexpectedly throughout the day. You can pair it with breathing, music, or positive thoughts, such as, "I am calm, I am safe, or I am loved." Once you feel calmer, you can then evaluate what your next step is in getting through the day. I personally like to pick one action item that I can manage that is a productive use of my time and is something I can actually control. Sometimes it just means cleaning out my car. Other times it means I make a phone call to the insurance agency. Maybe it means something big like working on an application for a new job. It can be anything of your choice, as long as it is you doing something that is a step toward either making the day productive and/or working toward the life you want to create for yourself.

Self-Care

We all have a variety of things we love to do, or that are restorative to our bodies and spirits. During trauma, we can't always provide the best self-care, but it is critical to begin practicing it in any little way possible, as soon as possible. We also need many ways to practice self-care. My favorite is walking at the ocean, but when I lived five hours from the nearest beach, it wasn't practical to wait six months to restore, so I had to fill in with other ways to take care of myself. I have included some self-care activities for you here, but please realize the possibilities are endless and be creative in finding what works for you. The important thing to remember is that you are doing it as a loving gesture to yourself, and to embrace that time as your own healing, as a gift from yourself.

Salt Soak

Though too much salt intake in our diets is not healthy, salt on our skin has a wide range of benefits. Salt soaks in warm water can draw out toxins and replenish nutrients as well as help to relax sore muscles. I recommend dead sea salts because they are so rich in nutrients. I often use Pink Himalayan salts as well. Epsom salts are popular and affordable and can help to draw out toxins, but are not as nutrient rich as sea salts. If you don't have access to a bathtub, you can fill a container and soak your feet. If you can visit the ocean, plan to get your feet wet in the surf or along the wet sand if possible. You can also fill a spray bottle with distilled water and the salt of your choice to mist onto your skin.

Remember that a very hot bath can dehydrate you and even pose health risks depending on conditions. Check in with your physician regarding salt soaks if you have any concerns. Hydrate with water before, during, and/or after your soak, especially if you break a sweat.

As with most of these techniques, the pairing of multiple strategies together can result in even more effective results. With my baths, I pair music or Tibetan chimes, positive thoughts, or a brief meditation to clear my mind. I am careful not to think about all of my responsibilities or worries during this time. Instead I fiercely protect it, knowing that it is renewing my energy so that I can keep moving forward.

Hydrate

Many of us forget to take care of basic needs during difficult times. Drinking plenty of water is needed to flush out the toxins that build up as a result of stress. Plan to flush those stress chemicals out by carrying a canteen of water with you at all times, and remind yourself to sip water throughout the day. Proper hydration is also needed for our minds to function correctly, which is important during times of stress. Many of the techniques listed here such as salt soaks and physical exercise can dehydrate us, so be aware that your body needs those fluids replenished to maintain physical and mental health processes. As you take a drink, be thinking positive and healing thoughts for your body. As you provide for your body, also provide for your mind and spirit, feeding it kind thoughts.

Crafts

My grandmother knits every single day. The first thing I asked to be donated to her was yarn and knitting needles. I was heartbroken over losing all of my beading and craft supplies, and overwhelmed with the thought of starting over. Finally, a supporter of a recovery group on Facebook sent me some beads, string, and needles. It was a small box that I could take with me anywhere and I didn't have to worry about storage space. I would sit on the bed or at the table in someone else's house and make healing bracelets. It took my mind off other things, and put my energies into something tangible and healthy. If crafts or building and tinkering work to ease your mind, try to find a way to use them even in little ways if you are putting your life back together.

Reading

Included with reading are audiobooks, which saved me both during my long term illness which impacted my vision, and again during the fire recovery process, when the boys and I shared a bed and I couldn't sleep but had to have the lights off. I also listened to them from my phone with earbuds the numerous times I was waiting in line at FEMA, which could take hours. Whatever form of books works for you can really be a needed diversion.

Reading can transport us to a completely different time or place, or both. This can be a much needed reprieve for us during difficult times. It can quiet our own thoughts by replacing those with the narrative of the author. Find a book that incorporates humor, encouraging words, or is entertaining enough to temporarily distract you.

Pets

If you don't have a pet and are well enough to care for one and can afford it, the benefits are significant. I had to wait two years before I could commit to being able to properly care for a pet. When I was finally able I got a little dog, my first pet as an adult. She has been a wonderful, loving companion, and loves to cuddle up next to me and my boys. On days that I don't feel well, she doesn't leave my side. Petting an animal is a great stress reliever, and can even lower blood pressure and cholesterol levels. They are also a preventative against loneliness, which is something to consider if you live alone or are alone for long periods of time and want companionship.

Additionally, dogs can be trained to be service animals to assist with many types of disabilities and are also very useful for practical purposes, such as alerting you to dangers. It is also very healthy for us to have something to care for, and pets can fill this need. For survivors who have to wait to get settled or who lost family pet members, I understand that the situation and timing has to be right. For supporters of survivors, there are still many pets from the Camp Fire waiting to be adopted from the shelters.

Essential Oils

It is estimated that the use of essential oils and botanicals have been in practice for at least 5,000 years and possibly longer. These practices paved the way for pharmacology and the use of medicinals for many types of healing. In recent years, the empirical research supporting the efficacy of essential oils and aromatherapy is quickly gaining momentum. Citrus oil can boost your mood, lavender can calm and help with sleep, and peppermint can increase concentration.

Topical application of essential oils can also significantly improve wellness and provide an alternate or complementary treatment plan for symptoms of grief, loss, and stress. Remember to check with your physicians regarding the topical/internal use of essential oils. Essential oils are highly concentrated and should be diluted with carrier oils to avoid irritation before putting them onto skin. It is always a good idea to test an area on your wrist to check for any irritation that may occur before using it in larger quantities on the body. For massage or a roller ball bottle, I blend mine with organic sunflower oil, which doesn't bother my sensitive skin and also has a good absorption rate. I also blend oils into an aloe vera gel base and rub it into my neck or temples. There are many carriers and endless essential oils that you can research and pair together for specific symptoms.

Blends are available from many oil companies as well as DIY recipes available online.

For aromatherapy, I have a small diffuser that humidifies the air while distributing essential oil. These are available for cars, or small personal areas with a USB cable, so even if you don't have a lot of space, you can make the best of the space you are in. I also blend oils into a small mister bottle with distilled water and a bit of sea salt to take with me when I travel around, and breathe it in when needed. There is also a lot of aromatherapy jewelry available now that people are using; lava beads or felt pads inserted into pendants absorb the oil and release the fragrance without topical use.

The internet is full of examples of essential oils and what they can treat. I recommend doing a search for "best essential oils + your symptom" and see what is suggested. If a particular oil smells really good to you, chances are it will be beneficial and a chemical match for your system. If something smells unappealing, I recommend looking for an alternate oil as there are many to choose from that can help to treat whatever symptoms you are experiencing.

Here are some examples to review: Lavender oil can treat headaches, tension, and stress. Chamomile has calming and soothing properties. Clary sage works as an antidepressant and can help alleviate anxiety. Smelling citrus is proven to boost mood and lower stress levels.

Be the Driver

I love this saying, and I use it in my classes with students every term. What it means is to be the driver on the road to your own destiny. If you are allowing others to determine your path, you are merely the passenger of your own life. I spent years in a job I didn't find rewarding, just going with the flow because administration got to make all the decisions. I spent years in a marriage that was disingenuous, allowing the relationship to drain my energy and positivity. I spent years swimming upstream against what was supposed to be my real path, fighting for things that were not worth fighting for. I began to feel resentful, beaten down, and lost. I needed to get back in the driver's seat. I made some serious changes regarding my thought processes. Every time I didn't get to contribute to a decision at work, I looked at grad schools. When a co-worker shared that my husband was seen out of town with another woman, I looked at attorneys. I used every bit of frustration, irritation, and pain to serve as a motivation to begin to create the life I wanted. After separating from my husband and two attempts at applying for a Master's program, I was accepted into a grad school for Clinical Psychology. I worked full time, had the boys full time, and they were two and five years old. My goal was to finish the three year program before they began to bring home history reports and science projects. It was so, so hard. But it was also the second most rewarding thing I have ever done, and I was creating a future life that would turn out to be more of a blessing than I had imagined possible. Every night when I worked on homework instead of watching television, every weekend when I wrote papers instead of meeting friends or dating, and every medical journal I read instead of reading a novel for recreation were conscious decisions to take action toward building my future.

It is no one else's responsibility to provide us with the life we want to have. It is no one else's responsibility to heal our pains and allow us to move on. If you are waiting on someone else to make your life right or to give you the life you deserve you might be waiting forever. If you keep living in that space of the passenger seat you will not end up where you want to be. Each day will give you the opportunity to take control of your life, your path, and work toward it one step at a time. Figure out what those small, medium, and big steps are and begin to take them. And when that giant leap of faith finally appears on your path, take that too.

Closing Note from the Author

Dear Readers:

What I want most for each of you is to begin making the decision, today, right now, to change how you manage and view your life by using some of the strategies discussed, or any techniques you have practiced in the past, that work for you as an individual. I wish for you to begin to see each day as a gift, as a blessing, as a chance to get one day closer to your dream life. It can be done! Practice positive thinking every single day, and use your energy on what you can change or accomplish, instead of dwelling on the past or negative thoughts. Focus on being the badass that got through it, that can lead others by example, and who will one day look back with awe on all that you survived. Use your energy to combat stress and make a plan. You won't always feel like it, but you can get through it. My thoughts and prayers are with you as you move forward into better times. You got this.

Dax

Acknowledgements

Thank you God, for the blessings, miracles, and love you have bestowed upon us. I am yours.

Our lives have been touched by thousands of hearts from around the world. If you contributed donations, supplies, time, housing, and prayers to survivors during and after the Camp Fire, I am forever grateful.

To CalFire and all of the firefighters who traveled from nearby states to risk your lives to save all of ours, there are no words of thanks great enough. You are my heroes.

To Dan The Teacher, I am so grateful to you for opening up your home to us and welcoming us in like family.

To my students, who encouraged me to take a leap of faith and share this story. Thank you for believing in me.

To my family, who always has my back, I love you and am so grateful for all of your support and love.

To my Andy, who put others before himself at such a young age in the face of danger; I could not be prouder. I love you so much.

And to my Tommy, who put aside fear and remembered to pray. I love you baby boy.

About the Author

Dax Meredith has a Master's Degree in Clinical Psychology with an emphasis on crisis counseling. Her research and training include PTSD and Veterans, suicide intervention, and increasing resiliency. Dax currently teaches and counsels students at the college level, and is working on another book about surviving long term illness. Her proudest accomplishment is being a mother. She lives in California with her two children and enjoys overcast days on the coast. This is her first book.

www.ingramcontent.com/pod-product-compliance
Lightning Source LLC
Chambersburg PA
CBHW020407080526
44584CB00014B/1218